I can't afford
to marry you

**A guide to understanding
the true cost of love**

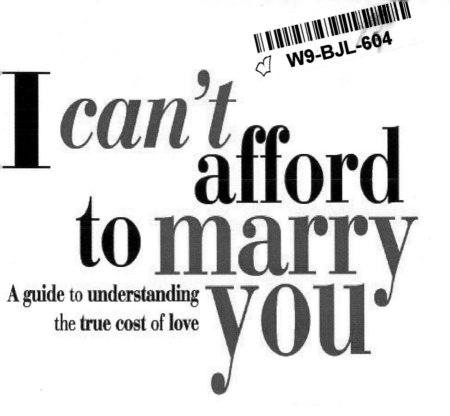

FOREWORD BY **LES BROWN**

MARILYN LOGAN

Please send your comments to the address below. Thank you in advance.
Salo Publishing
5925 Kirby
Suite E454
Houston, Texas 77005

I Can't Afford To Marry You

Requests for information should be addressed to:
5925 Kirby
Suite E454
Houston, Texas 77005

For more information, about Marilyn, or for seminars and speaking engagements, please visit www.marilynlogan.com or call (713)748-0540. For answers concerning any questions you may have about money, please contact Marilyn via her email address: marilyn@marilynlogan.com.

ISBN - 0-9777271-0-6

Printed in the United States of America.

This book is designed to provide general information about finance. It is sold with the understanding that the publisher, author and advisors are not rendering counseling or other professional services. Every effort has been made to make this book as complete and accurate as possible, however, this text should be used only as a general guide and not as the ultimate source of information on finance, credit, stocks or real estate investing.

Contributing writer: Cedrick Smith, M.D.
Cover design: StudioMarc Creative.
Book production: mybestseller.com

WHAT People are saying about "I Can't Afford to Marry You."

Your book made me reflect on so many things from my past and even more on how to improve my future. I will never look at my potential mate the same after reading your book.

- **Karlin Davine**

Your fiancé would risk losing you to help you find yourself. I've never had that experience...It's nice to know that unselfish people like that really exist.
- **Carlton Champion**

If I ever feel myself slipping into my old financial habits, I will read it again as a reminder that I can and will do better!

- **Gwen Donaldson**

Your tip, "Always keep a side hustle," was right on point. Reading that made me adamant about not giving up on my little candle company.

- **Renee Talmer**

You have "hit the nail on the head". I never could put my finger on it before I read your book, but I now realize that a couple of my friends' marriages are on the verge of disaster over money issues; I will be giving them a copy of your book.
- **Terry Wilkins**

This book should be a requisite read for singles and those that may be considering a serious relationship/marriage. It sets a simple base of financial principles to avoid financial disaster later.

- **Wilma Brown**

I was a near emotional wreck when I finished the book. Although a quick read, I laughed, coughed, cried, cheered and gasped all the way through!
- **Frank Albertson**

Your book touches many emotions, financial experiences and relationship challenges faced by people of yesteryear and in modern society. You can never be too educated about money!

- **Victoria Williams**

Table Of Contents

Dedication

To the love of my life:

My son

JOHN WESLEY LOGAN III (TREY)

Acknowledgments

GOD – For leading John to me.

JOHN WESLEY LOGAN, JR – For being a kind, considerate and loving husband. It's because of you that I am at this place.

SON - JOHN WESLEY LOGAN III – You are the reason I awake every morning. I wish you would have known your Dad – you truly are so much like him.

MOM, MARY ARRINGTON – I'm more like you than you'll ever know.

MOTHER-IN-LAW – MARTHA LOGAN – Thanks for raising a wonderful son, who became a fabulous husband.

BUSINESS PARTNER – CYNTHIA CHAMPION – Thanks for your friendship, love and perseverance.

FRIEND – TONGELA CLARK – God sent you to protect me.

FRIEND – KATHY SAPP – I think you really are my sister. Sure feels like it.

FRIEND – TERA ROBERSON – Your hip style gave me flavor.

FRIEND – LEVI BENTON – For loving my son.

FRIEND – GWEN DANIELS – Your support and love has been consistent.

FRIEND – ALLISON NEAL – Virgos unite when need be.

FRIEND – TERRY BESSARD – Thanks for all of your input and hard work.

FRIEND – CEDRICK SMITH – Thanks for asking me the motivating question "Why don't you want to finish the book?" Your support, creativity, insight and hours of contributions will always be greatly appreciated. You kept me laughing and allowed me to be sad.

Foreword

Money. Everybody wants it. Most can't manage it. In *I Can't Afford to Marry You*, Marilyn Logan shares her very personal experience in financial irresponsibility and its effect on her life. Her journey from financial ignorance to financial literacy is an amazing one. Like many of us, she grew up in a family where making ends meet was a struggle and getting necessities – much less wants – often was out of the question. That leant itself to an early adulthood of overspending, relying on credit, and ignoring her growing money hassle.

But her money woes also leant themselves to something else: an entrepreneurial spirit. At times that leaning did not pay off – you'll find the story of her ill fated hot-dog stand interesting. But sometimes, it did pay off – and in a big way: check out her story about the penny stock she bought that netted her family a nice return.

Each of these stories, while entertaining, worked an even greater benefit for Logan: experience. And it's that experience she shares with her readers in this open, honest and poignant memoir.

Like Marilyn – and many of you – I was raised wanting more for myself. Through hard work – and more than a few mistakes – I was able to finally define my own future. That led me to making good financial decisions and attaining financial stability by creating a multi-million dollar speaking enterprise. Many of the lessons I learned, I've also found repeated in Marilyn's book.

Whether you want to finally be honest about your own financial circumstance, or whether you want to know what mistakes to avoid on your way to financial independence, this is a book you must read. Marilyn Logan does a delightful job of mixing personal experience with practical tools to create a solid foundation.

Let her help you get out of your financial hole.

— Les Brown, award winning speaker
and best selling author

CHAPTER 1

Until Debt Do Us Part

Liability is not a word you often come across in preparing for what is billed as the happiest day of your life; it is however a word that nearly became an insurmountable stumbling block in my life. I was 19, and although I knew what liability meant, I never considered myself to be a liability. Yet that's where I was, the blushing bride to be with my own scarlet letter L.

I was supposed to be getting married, and after months of harried and meticulous preparation, everything was set up. I booked the reception hall, the honeymoon to San Francisco was arranged, the bridesmaids' pastel-colored dresses - representing the colors of the rainbow - were hanging in their respective closets, and the groomsmen tuxedos, rumored to move the proudest of penguins to jealousy, were patiently awaiting their stunning debut. The wedding invitations had been sent and the RSVPs were coming in at a rate that assured that the sanctuary would be full of well-wishers witnessing our blessed event. The wedding was only one month away and all my dashing groom and I had left to do was coast and enjoy the precious time we had together.

One would assume bliss, right? The mortification and pronouncement of me being a liability stopped me and my wedding day plans dead in my tracks. Why? How? Liability? I was a complement to this man; the ying to his yang, the Juliet to his Romeo, the sugar to his Kool-Aid. How could I be anything, but a bonus to his life?

To my surprise, John decided to look at my finances, and what he saw was a deep gaping hole that I dug for myself.

It was Saturday afternoon. A few hours earlier, I picked up John from Chicago O'Hare International Airport, a regular every-other-week routine since his job had transferred him to Bismarck, North Dakota. He was sitting at the kitchen table, the place of light discussions and serious meals. I knew I had at least one thing ready for our marriage; I definitely knew how to cook. John sat at the table with the rigidity of a man coming to terms with his end. It is said the way to a man's heart is through his stomach, but I was quickly realizing that the way out of this man's heart was through his wallet.

There are certain moments in life that you never forget. I will always remember how John looked at me, firm and direct. I had little time to comprehend this unfamiliar and increasingly uncomfortable gaze. Unsure of this emotional place, I was broadsided, and the blow nearly floored me when he said, **"I can't afford to marry you. The wedding is off. You are a liability."**

I was judged and affixed with the moniker of "Liability." A liability! I thought, "How am I a liability?" Webster says a liability is *1. An obligation or duty. 2. Something for which one is liable. 3. A debt.* [And the worst.] *4. Something that works as a disadvantage.* He had to have his t-accounts wrong, if anything I was an asset. I was dumb struck.

I was confused about a lot of things at that particular moment, but I was also young and oblivious to the powerful influences finance and money would have on my life; my rapidly evaporating married life. John was saying I was a disadvantage! I thought to myself, "How did I suddenly become a disadvantage?" We argued back and forth, hour after hour- to no avail. He was saying I was a financial liability that he couldn't afford.

I didn't even believe that this was about money. How could money get in the way of true love? I thought there must be another woman or maybe he was getting cold feet; I could handle that better. However, this liability finance thing was foreign. I just couldn't understand why this was an issue.

John's resolve was strong and never weakened. It was like I was in a daze. I felt hurt and baffled. I could tell he knew the state of my emotions, yet his determination never wavered. After a while I became numb. I was devoid of any next steps, an unusual position for someone whose survival skills had been honed on the south side of Chicago. My Chicago street smarts had let me down. He really meant it. He couldn't afford to marry me because I would be a financial liability.

He stated his position in the cold, unyielding manner of a banker rejecting your loan application.

"When I marry you, I marry your debt. When I marry you, I will be marrying your credit report to my credit report. I don't want to merge my credit report with your credit. You have too much debt. You're too big of a risk, and your risky spending behavior may cost us too much money and could ultimately breakup our marriage."

That's when I broke down and tears started to flow. They were honest tears, but I knew they could be used as leverage against him. What man can resist the tear stained face of a woman broken? After 45 minutes of theatrics and humiliation, he still hadn't budged, and it became clear to me that I had to develop another strategy. My thoughts turned to saving face before my family and friends. I wondered how do I tell everyone that the wedding is off? John had already bought us a house, but now there would be no wedding, and possibly no relationship. So I gave up on the feminine strategy and asked him bluntly, "What do you want from me? What can I do to continue with our wedding plans?"

He simply replied, "I'm not interested in marrying anyone who can't handle money. Marilyn, what I'm trying to get you to understand is that the wedding itself is only a day, a marriage is a lifetime. I know we are best friends. We have a lot in common and we are spiritually yoked, but we are simply not financially yoked." I wanted to kick him in the yokes! That was rock bottom. No wedding, no house, no man, nothing. I walked out of the room, fearing I might break down again or else visit serious violence on this man I still wanted so badly. Finally, in utter desperation, I walked into the kitchen and asked, as calmly as I could,

"Is there any way this can be worked out? Is there anything I can say or do to cause this wedding to be back on?"

He looked at me, and with a cool expression that said he would brook no disagreement on the issue, said, "I want your credit cards."

I was shocked. "My credit cards!? Not my credit cards!" How dare he demand what I took pride in owning? Those credit cards gave me strength, power and a sense of establishment. Had he gone mad?

Again, he looked at me and said, "I want your credit cards, all of them." I was quickly realizing that the man of my dreams, in an instant, was becoming the man of my reality! And, John the "reality-man" wasn't playing around.

His purpose was clear and I knew that if we were going to have a wedding, I had to do as he asked. As I began to retrieve them, I noticed that I had carefully hidden them in different compartments - making it impossible to keep track of how much credit I was actually using. I was like an alcoholic hiding bottles around the house. There were credit cards in my purse, but many found their way into nooks and crannies not often visited by light. That was the point, of course. He was right - I had a problem. I knew it, but I wasn't prepared to admit it to myself. I reluctantly pulled the credit cards out from their hiding places, one by one, I think in all there may have been 13 or 15. I threw them on the table in front of him. "Here. That's all of them."

He now had all of my cards. John then asked for the statements. A piece of plastic is one thing; it's anonymous in what it represents, but the statements? The statements were the cold, hard reality of my debts. I didn't want to reveal the statements to him because I feared his response to how much I really owed. Why couldn't he just leave well enough alone? He was sitting still, in a slightly forward position. His eyes stared at me from his handsome, dark face, which just a short while ago had been laughing and smiling. He waited for my response. As I was searching for answers, I only thought of ways to distract him. I tried rubbing his back, kissing his cheeks and offering him sex. I stalled. "What did you say, honey?" I tried to distract him by offering up dinner at our favorite restaurant and even more sex. He would not be moved. The intense focus that was a hallmark of his work as an engineer was now being metered out in our relationship. I had never seen him quite like this before. Again, I had to surrender the evidence that would incriminate me.

Like a kid having been sent to go get the switch for his own spanking, I walked slowly into the bedroom where the credit card statements were neatly hidden and walked out even slower. John might as well have asked me to take off all of my clothes at halftime of a Bears game. I felt exposed.

The credit cards made a small heap on the table. The room became quiet except for the sound of envelopes opening, statements unfolding and clicks of calculator keys adding up my debt. Like a prosecutor, he peppered me with questions.

"How much do you pay Sears per month?"

I mumbled incoherently.

"How much do you pay Marshall Fields per month?"

I mumbled even more.

"How much do you ... ?"

"I only pay the minimum amount," I finally said, agitated with his incessant questioning.

"Every month?" he inquired with an incredulous look on his face; the first hint of an emotional reaction since this whole sordid conversation began.

"Yes! Whatever the minimum amount is, I pay," I answered, a little quieter.

"Marilyn," he said, picking up a $600.00 bill, "do you have any idea how long it will take to pay this off? Do you know how much paying $9.00 a month at 19% interest adds up to? It's going to take you over 10 years to pay this off." His voice seemed more grave with each "Do you know?"

"I don't know," I said with a wail. "Stop badgering me," I pleaded. "Let's talk about this in the bedroom," I said enticingly.

John would not be swayed. He went back to my pile of debt. "Marilyn, how are you living? Where is your money going?" He didn't know how much I was making as an administrative assistant, so I told him.

"Marilyn, you don't make enough to live the way you live."

"What do you mean, 'I don't make enough money'?"

"You are living above your means," he said.

I was shocked when he added up all of my debt because the total was a staggering $11,124.58! I was 19-years-old and over $11,000.00 in debt! Calmly, he pulled his checkbook out of his back pocket, and wrote a check for $11,124.58. I couldn't believe it when he wrote my name on the check, but then he looked me in the eyes sternly and instructed me, in no uncertain terms, that on Monday morning, no later than 10 o'clock, I was to pay off every one of my creditors. I was filled with a mixture of relief and indignation. The burden of debt was lifted, but he was treating me like a child, which, I admitted later, is how I was behaving with credit cards.

He didn't just stop there. As John sat there cutting up every one of *my* credit cards, he said, "Marilyn, we can't manage our finances your way, it won't work. It's a prescription for disaster and our marriage will not last." Snip, snip went the scissors; cutting up the credit cards. With each cut, he was shredding my dignity. "There are many battles in marriage and I don't want money issues to turn into a war between us."

My insides were boiling. I felt as if he was trying to control me. I had to swallow my pride. Pride is the stuff that gets caught in your throat, cutting off the oxygen supply to your brain thus causing irrational thinking. You can find yourself going deeper and deeper into a horrible situation because you won't do *what's necessary* to pull yourself out.

P.R.I.D.E, **P**remarital **R**easons **I**t **D**ied **E**arly, almost cost me the love of my life.

Logan's Lessons

Before starting a serious relationship, exchange credit reports and AIDS tests. The former will reveal past and present spending habits. The latter will reveal the obvious. Love is more than pecks on the cheeks and public displays of affection. One should give equal value to the financial aspects of your partner as you do with the love aspects. Don't go into a serious relationship financially out of shape.

My advice is:

- Learn to live within your means.

- Reduce your credit card debt quickly. Interest rates wait for no one.

- You should only have one or two credit cards.

- At least check your credit report yearly at www.annualcreditreport.com; the first report is free.

- Ignorance can be bliss, but it can also be very costly! Wise up!

CHAPTER 2

Food Or Fashion;
What's A Girl To Do?

I grew up on Aberdeen Street on the south side of Chicago. I lived there with my mother, father, two brothers and three sisters. My parents owned the two story walk-up we lived in. I thought it was cool that my mom got money from the tenant (her sister) who lived on the first floor, every month; well, maybe not every month. I learned that you have to be cautious when renting to family; they generally have excuses as to why they can't pay, or why they are short. Further, like my mother, people are often times lenient toward their family when collecting rent.

The one good thing about having family living below us was there were always plenty of family around, enough that we didn't have to invite other people to our birthday parties. All you had to do was grab the kids from the top and the bottom floors, call a few cousins, and we had a party. We did practically everything together; shopping, going to the movies and even attending church. In fact, if our family didn't show up, there was no church. Even with such a large family, immediate or otherwise, I never felt like I really fit in.

None of my siblings were like me. I often asked my mom if I was adopted; I knew that I wasn't. I looked just like her and sometimes shared the same personality and mannerisms. I couldn't understand how my siblings and I could have the same parents, eat the same food, take a bath in the same bathtub - and sometimes in the same bathwater - and be so different. It wasn't just in my home that I was different. My relatives, schoolmates, and even my minister singled me out as "that girl."

In the summer months, I rarely played outside during the daylight hours like most kids. I thought it made more sense to play when the sun went down and was cooler. Why be miserable while you played - all sweaty and stuff? I didn't mind playing by myself. It was as if I was in my own little world. Sometimes my adventures with imaginary friends were more memorable than anything I could have done with my siblings or cousins.

Coming from a household where we struggled to make ends meet, we could barely pay for our needs - let alone my wants. Being somewhat of a "girly-girl," I wanted new clothes. Instead I was outfitted with hand-me-downs from my sisters. Asking my mother for money was out of the question and I was too young to get a job. I earned money by doing odd jobs in the neighborhood: painting railings and stairs, ironing clothes and cleaning flower beds. I may have been a girly-girl, but I was resourceful.

People were always ready to offer their opinions as to who I was. I didn't think I was more special than anyone else, but I did do things that made sense to me, even if it meant going against the grain. I had a lot of confidence and sass; I felt as though I was a special little girl. I was resourceful, independent, and with a girly appetite – a formula for creating a sense of entitlement. This developing sense of entitlement is one of the things that got me so deep into debt.

My mother was a strict disciplinarian, because my dad was never around. She managed the family as best she could. She was the one person I did not want to disappoint and was everything to me: provider, mother, comforter and cheerleader. Fear of my mother motivated me, and also protected me from going down the wrong path. However, there were times when my mother needed to be protected. After she divorced my father, my mother had a long relationship with a man who was sometimes really sweet and gentle. Unfortunately, he was possessed by a demon - alcohol. When he mixed alcohol with anger, he would lose self-control and become physically abusive. More than a few times, the Chicago Police Department had to dispatch officers to our home because of domestic disturbances.

During one of his drinking episodes, I heard a lot of commotion coming from my mother's bedroom. I rushed in and saw him hitting her. I started kicking and punching him to no avail. He easily brushed me aside and flung me to the floor. I could see the rage in his eyes. He looked totally out of control. I grabbed the car keys out of my mother's purse and ran to the car parked out front as fast as I could.

Underage and unlicensed, I drove the car to my uncle's house to get his rifle; I knew he always kept it hidden in the hall closet. I made up a quick lie as I approached the door. I said to my uncle, without a hint of desperation in my voice, "Mom needs some milk and eggs for a cake." When he turned his back to retrieve the items, I made a mad dash for the closet and grabbed the rifle. The next thing I recall was seeing my uncle's house in the rear view mirror as I sped for home.

I sat quietly in the hallway at the base of the stairs with the rifle waiting for my mother's abuser to come downstairs. The rifle was heavy and my hands began to sweat. I could hear the blood pumping in my ears as seconds ticked by. There was a coppery taste in my mouth and I couldn't feel my feet. I resolved that I would protect my mother from this man. I waited undeterred for him to come out. Fortunately for both him and me, he had already left, and the confrontation was averted. Otherwise, I may have written another kind of book – from behind bars.

My family didn't encourage college after I graduated from high school, but I was determined to go. I didn't understand all of the mechanics of college, but I knew whatever I didn't comprehend about higher education, I needed to learn. I didn't even know what I wanted to do. My earlier dream of becoming a dentist had been shattered by a high school counselor who informed me that such a career was out of my reach.

I registered for four night courses at Kennedy-King College in Chicago. Coupled with my course load, I continued to work at my now full-time job for the water district downtown during the day. I had been working at this job since my senior year of high school as part of a co-op program. This was a totally different challenge for me; working part-time and taking high school classes was one thing, but working full-time and taking a full load of college courses was another. Frankly, I was afraid, but I was determined to become college educated and successful.

Initially, my job at the water district was just an entry-level position, but before long I was promoted to a full time administrative assistant in the legal department, which came with an increase in pay. It was my first real office job and it opened the door for my first official taste of adulthood. Unfortunately, it also introduced me to the lure of credit cards.

My financial life – struggling but getting by – and behavior were about to change; like how the Titanic had a "change" of course after hitting that big iceberg. As an administrative assistant, I often accompanied my boss and other co-workers to various business meetings and lunches. I distinctly recall my boss and co-workers using their credit cards to pay the bills. I thought this was cool and made them look important and powerful. I wanted to feel important too!

I was a full-time employee and a college student. In my mind I had it going on, but if I was going to fit in like my co-workers, I felt I had to have a new car. I didn't know much about the car buying process, but I knew I wanted a new car. In fact, in my warped perception, I needed a new car to be successful.

I went to the local dealership all dressed up in my Sunday finest. I remember a well-dressed man approaching me and asking in a southern drawl, "How you doing little lady? What you lookin' for?"

"A new car." I replied confidently. He assured me that today was my lucky day. He showed me a white Vega with red interior. "Ooooh," I said to myself. I want this car. It was sharp. "I'll take it!"

He quickly handed me the papers to sign and I obliged. I foolishly paid full sticker price. I was probably his easiest sale of the day, most likely of his career. I didn't ask the salesman one question. I was just grateful to be a new car "owner."

What a sucker! I was elated that they gave me a radio - I didn't know radios came with cars. I was shocked that they left a tire in the trunk - I didn't know spare tires came with cars, either. Okay, by now it's clear I knew nothing about buying a car, let alone owning one.

The car sat in front of my mother's house most times. The expenses of maintaining a car were difficult. I couldn't afford parking and would take the bus and train to get to work downtown, but I was proud to tell people I owned a new car. I drove it only on weekends.

Enjoying my new-found independence, I thought it was time for me to get my own place. My mother thought 19 was too young to be on my own, and she felt I was biting off more than I could chew. Having a new job and new car, it didn't feel right living with my mother in her three bedroom house.

In my eyes, I was an adult and it was time for me to take on adult responsibilities. I found a studio apartment right off Michigan Avenue. It had a beautiful view of Lake Michigan. The cool, stylish and young people lived in this part of Chicago. The apartment manager told me that he had many people who wanted the apartment; he asked me what I could give him "extra" if he allowed me to rent the unit. I may have been financially naïve and an easy mark, but I wasn't a dummy. I told him he would get the rent on time and that was all he could expect from me. The only "extra" available to him would be a clean apartment when I moved out. I immediately had the locks changed when I moved in.

This was the beginning of me living life in the fast lane. I was a college student, had a full-time job, a new car, lived a few blocks from Lake Michigan, and had a little money in my pocket. I had it all! I was always shopping for new clothes, buying furnishings for my apartment, and collecting credit cards like little girls collect baby dolls. If I didn't have the cash for something, I simply put it on a credit card. My motto was "spend at all cost."

I was quickly gathering debt, but I never really felt any adverse affects. All I felt was the satisfaction of instant gratification. All those things I wanted when I was young were mine now. I felt like I was hip. I felt like I was with it. I felt like I had it going on.

If I saw something I wanted, I could have it. My friends and relatives envied me because it appeared as if I had it all. My lifestyle was being paid for with borrowed money. I was only paying the minimum payments on my credit cards. I was late a couple of times on my rent, but just juggled a few things around and got it paid. I recall my landlord knocking on my door a few times. I would sit quietly in the bathroom afraid to face him. My promise to pay him on time was turning out to be a lie. I didn't realize that looking important was so expensive.

At my mom's house, I was accustomed to having family around sharing in the living expenses. Things were tight and getting tighter, but I didn't want to admit to my mother, much less myself, that I was digging myself into a hole. I had too much pride. Something had to be cut out of my budget and the only thing I could think of was food. In the hierarchy of food, shelter and warmth, I put food below shopping. I unplugged my refrigerator to save on electricity and consequently had to develop a plan of eating. I figured I had enough relatives that I could visit on a regular basis and fill my stomach. Every Monday I would visit my Aunt Maeola's house around dinnertime. We would sit in her kitchen and chat, while the aroma of collard greens filled the air. Then, I would offer to clean her kitchen and put away her food.

"Aunt Maeola," I would ask, "do you want me to put this food away for you?"

"Would you baby?"

I gladly put it away - in my mouth and in storage containers. And so it went, the same plot played out at different relatives' homes throughout the week. It's how I ate for free and maintained my lifestyle.

Logan's Lessons

Trying to live the celebrity lifestyle has become more of the norm for people. Unfortunately, the "norm" does not have celebrity income. The average adult age 25-34 spends $.25 of every $1.00 earned on debt payments. This age group also has the second highest rate of bankruptcy.

My advice is:

- Learn from your financial mistakes; you will make them!

- Use what you own! Do you really need 20 pairs of jeans or 30 dress shirts?

- Don't use credit cards to supplement your salary or pay for a lifestyle you can't afford.

- Pay for your needs. Save for your wants.

- Learn early that money matters.

CHAPTER 3

Do You Take This Debt To Be Your Lawfully Wedded Wife?

I'd been living on my own for about eight months and making it okay – if you overlook that little bit about my rotating family mooching – when I first saw John Wesley Logan II in a crowd. Actually, I saw the back of his head and even from that angle I thought, "Wow, he's cute." He was tall and handsome with a successful corporate look. It was the end of a workday and while most people were making their way home, I was on my way to class. I didn't have time to flirt.

I cut through the Prudential Plaza Building to avoid the cold and ended up in the Randolph Street Station, where some of the crowd took the subway and others got on the elevated train. I cut through three more buildings and somehow, the man whom

I was admiring earlier was walking beside me. He asked me my name, and I immediately put up a Chicago Bears like defense - I had an "I don't know you, you're a stranger" look on my face. Plus, I wasn't dressed right to meet him. I thought I had the skinniest legs and the longest neck. I only wanted to meet guys when I had on a turtleneck and pants. (It's a girl thing.) Additionally, I was dating an older guy named Michael, although it wasn't serious. In a relationship, receiving gifts was important to me. While we were dating, he refused to acknowledge my birthday or Christmas with a gift. In my mind, Michael and I were about over.

Despite my personal dilemmas and the dramas playing in my head, John and I started talking. We boarded the same train and before the ride was done, we exchanged phone numbers. I was smitten. Not only was he tall and handsome, he was also engaging and interesting. I was hopeful that he would call that night, but he didn't. I never called a guy, ever, but, once in a while the universe instructs you to step out of your comfort zone. That night I broke my rule and called the "train man" - John. After two rings, a woman answered the phone. I was shocked, but I held it together and asked to speak to John. When he answered, I immediately asked, with a slightly jealous tone, "Who was that woman?"

"My mother," he answered.

I breathed a sigh of relief.

Our first date was set for Valentine's Day. John worked full-time as a civil engineer and was working on his master's degree at University of Chicago in the evenings. He planned to arrive at my place after his last class. I didn't have class that night, so I went straight home to prepare the only thing that was easy to make and guaranteed to be tasty - spaghetti.

As I was preparing for John's arrival, my soon-to-be ex-boyfriend, Michael, called. He said he had something for me and wanted to come over. I asked, "What is it?" When Michael said a card, I told him to keep the card and give it to his mother and hung up. A few minutes later, John appeared at my door with a dozen yellow roses and a bottle of wine. All I could say was, "Come on in." The rest, as they say, is history.

He wined me, dined me and romanced me off my feet. He was generous, funny and confident. Our first true confrontation came that day he told me that he couldn't afford to marry me. I later realized that some of that anger I had over him telling me I had to get rid of my credit cards and reform my spending habits was born of seeing that creep who was so abusive with my mother. John wasn't that guy. He was the man I loved, respected truly cherished, and he gave me my first lesson in financial responsibility.

We overcame our near deal breaking "affording me issue," and we were married at Lighthouse Baptist Church in Chicago. It was a wonderful wedding. Over 200 of our best friends, relatives and well-wishers sent us into life with hopes and dreams for a beautiful future together.

We returned from our honeymoon to start a new life. After just a few weeks, we moved to Bismarck, North Dakota. This wouldn't be the first time in our lives that John's work would cause us to relocate on short notice. On the surface our marriage looked fine. We were newlyweds, happily in love and had our financial priorities in order! What could possibly be wrong? I had to prove to John that I was an equal partner when it came to our finances. I wanted to repay him every cent of the $11,124.58 he gave me to pay off my credit card debt. No matter what it took, whatever sacrifices I would have to make, I was going to do it. I just had to keep my efforts a secret.

When John cut up my credit cards, he cut up some of my ego, my dignity, and a part of my self-esteem. I needed to get them back in order to feel good about myself in our relationship. I wanted to prove to him my financial value. I still had some insecurity about being labeled a financial liability. I felt like I was an employee trying to impress my new employer. I was determined to demonstrate that I could be a worthy asset to the success of our marriage financially.

I was resolute in carrying out my plan. We were living solely off of John's salary and his expense account. His company paid for our apartment, the groceries, and all of our utilities. They also gave him a company car, which meant we didn't have a car payment. This meant we didn't have to worry about any living expenses. Financially speaking, there was no need for me to work. From John's point of view this was a perfect scenario. We would have plenty of time to bond as newlyweds. However, I thought it was a perfect time for other reasons. It was a great opportunity for me to get a job, save my money, and repay John. This would allow me to regain my financial dignity. I knew John wouldn't understand, but I had to tell him I needed a job

One night over dinner I found myself feeling especially brave. "Honey, I'm going to look for a job tomorrow."

"Why do you need a job?" he asked.

"I've always worked John, ever since I was a little kid. I enjoy working."

I tried to comfort him by saying "I know I don't have to work but I want to." Deep down, I knew I needed an income. I needed money!

After days and weeks of job hunting I was beginning to believe I couldn't find work in this small town, at least not the type of work I wanted. Out of desperation, I took a job as a waitress in a restaurant that was part of a small upscale hotel close to the airport. I made $1.15 an hour. However, the tips were huge! I used my pretty smile, warm personality, and the novelty that I was one of two Black people in Bismarck – John was the other one. I started to make $60 to $70 in tips a night! I was working the dinner shift in the restaurant from 5:30 to 10:30, three or four days a week and I was saving all my tips. Unfortunately, John didn't enjoy the evening absence of his new bride, if you catch my meaning. His feelings had to be put on hold - at least for the time being, while I restored my self-esteem, self-respect and kept sight of my goal.

My tips went to the bank every morning. "Out of sight - out of mind," was my motto. I figured if I couldn't see the money, I wouldn't spend it. Besides, this way John wouldn't know and I could watch the total grow.

It didn't take too long before I realized that it was going to take me quite a while to save $11,124.58. I accumulated quite a bit of money in a few weeks, but I was eager to accomplish my mission of repaying John in six months. I needed to pay this debt back to my husband and it was going to take much longer than I had anticipated. So I woke up one morning and announced, "I need to find another job."

John's response was, "That's great!" He was so agreeable because he thought that I was going to take a day job so that I could be home with him at night. My heart was heavy with the thoughts of him missing me, but nothing was going to stop me from my agenda.

"Oh, no, baby! I'm keeping my night job. I need to find another job, a *day* job. I've got to have another job just so I can have something to do! My days are empty." A cloud of confusion crossed over John's face as he tried to come to terms with what I was saying.

It's rare to find a man who knows when to let his wife do what she wants without a quarrel. John was wise, and seemed to accept his lonely fate, or so I thought.

I contacted an employment agency and they helped me find a job at a law firm from noon to 5:00 p.m., this arrangement worked out nicely with my evening shift in the restaurant.

I was familiar with the law firm environment and enjoyed my work. Well, things were going as planned. I was saving my tips from the restaurant, and now I was saving the money I was making at the law firm. I was a lean, mean, money saving machine, and I must admit, it was taking a toll on my marriage.

"Where's my *wife?*" John used to ask me at odd moments, like when I was going out the door to one of my jobs. I thought he was nuts - I was right there in front of him! But then I got it. It was becoming obvious to me that I'd better get the money paid back to him before he ran out of patience! One morning I woke up and had an epiphany. I said to myself, "This isn't working fast enough. I need another job!" When I walked into the bathroom that morning, I think I frightened my husband. I must have had a look of total determination on my face, and that startled him. Curious, he looked at me and asked, "What are you doing up so early?"

I said, "Honey, I need to find another job." As he looked at me, his expression quickly changed into a frown. He had heard this one before. He looked away, shook his head as if to clear his mind of the remnants of a bad dream and walked into the bedroom to get dressed. He didn't say a word. Later, over breakfast, John seemed lost in thought. I suspected he was making an earnest attempt to understand just what I was really trying to tell him. John was an engineer, and it was his nature to analyze. It didn't take long.

"What are you talking about, 'find another job'? You have two jobs already! How could you possibly need three jobs?" After waiting a few moments he knew I wasn't going to answer him. Exasperated he asked, "Okay, what's going on here? Are you seeing somebody?"

"Are you kidding me?" I replied.

I had to put a stop to this line of questioning. I had my secret safely tucked away inside of me, and I had to protect it at all costs. I was determined to repay John and I would not waver. Very calmly I said to him, "But I don't have anything to do between the hours of 8:00 in the morning and 12:00 noon! So I plan to look for another job!"

"Where?" he asked.

"I don't know, but what I do know is that somebody will hire me today! I can promise you that!"

I got dressed, made myself look fabulous, jumped into my car, and began driving all around town trying to find employment – that day. Not tomorrow, or next week, that day. I found myself pulling up in front of Bismarck Hospital. I thought, *"Wait a minute. This is a hospital and hospitals have to be open 24 hours a day, seven days a week, right?"*

I knew they must have some type of work waiting for me inside. The human resources manager and I had a lengthy conversation and during some part of that dialogue she asked me if I could type and spell. There was a part-time position that called for those skills. I could type 70-75 words per minute, but I really was not a good speller; I couldn't spell my way out of a 6th grade classroom. I lied enthusiastically, "Of course' I can spell!" I even went so far as to tell her that I had entered spelling bees in elementary school. "Why in middle school, I was so good, I went on to the State Spelling Bee Contest!" The lies flowed as fast as I could speak; I had to have this job!

I was assigned to the medical records department; if ever you were a doctor or a patient at Bismarck Hospital, I apologize to you.

I was transcribing medical records for in-patients and surgeries. Can you imagine? I was so lost in the beginning. I didn't know if there were two t's in vomit or one. I had all types of dictionaries surrounding me at all times. I delayed no telling how many procedures. I couldn't transcribe the intake information fast enough. I was constantly being ridiculed by my peers, but eventually I became proficient at my position. I eventually worked my way up to being a transcriber trainer. I learned that regardless of what challenges you may be presented in life, you have to stick to your guns and persevere. When you are on a mission, I believe it is okay to fake it, to make it. In my opinion, this was one of those times in my life.

There I was working three jobs. The time away was quite difficult and for the first few months of marriage, I really never saw my husband; other than great sex here and there, and a shared cup of coffee on some mornings. We were like ships passing in the night. While John was working to secure our financial future, I was on a mission to regain my financial dignity.

Logan's Lessons

There are really only two ways to affect your financial bottom line – either make more money or decrease your expenses. If a second job or third job is required to cut your debt, do what you have to do. Short term pain can lead to long term gain. When you respect your money, your money will respect you.

My advice is:

- Get an understanding of your own behavior and feelings about money.

- Pay off your highest interest credit card debt first.

- Openly discuss your financial obligations with your spouse.

- Look at your marriage as a financial merger and assess your role in keeping financial harmony in your partnership.

- Take your financial goals seriously or risk losing your relationship over something frivolous.

CHAPTER 4

Lie Ability

It was another frigid North Dakota winter night and I told John I was taking him out to dinner to celebrate me quitting one of my jobs. The truth was, I had an ulterior motive. John had helped me reshape the way I thought about money, debt, finances and liabilities. He fundamentally reshaped how I ordered my financial affairs, and he put up with my increasingly workaholic lifestyle since we'd moved. It was time to reward him.

After dinner we shared a delicious slice of cheesecake, and we were sitting back enjoying the afterglow. I reached inside my purse and I pulled out a neatly wrapped gift box. He opened the card which read, "I'm no longer a liability and I love you for being honest with me." Inside the box was a check for $11,124.58. I had it all, to the penny. He couldn't have been more shocked if it had been the Hope Diamond.

"Honey!" he said to me, "You didn't have to do this!"

I watched him settle back into his chair with a sense of satisfaction and accomplishment that made me warm inside. The silence hung in the air like a cloud. He looked up at me with his kind loving eyes, "We are husband and wife, what's mine is yours and what's yours, is mine." He reached out, held my hand in his, and gently kissed my wedding ring.

Until this moment, in a legal sense, what was his was ours and what was mine was mine. But only after I gave him the check was it real to me. He didn't want to take the check. I explained to him that my false sense of self-esteem had been torn apart with each credit card he destroyed, and that only by earning the money to pay him back could I fill that empty place with real self-esteem. I told him that I needed to have a financial voice in our financial relationship and I didn't feel like I would be heard when money matters were decided if I was a debtor to him.

He was taken aback by my comments. "Besides," I said, knowing that feminine wiles are never out of order, "You're such a generous and loving husband that in a month or two you will probably treat me with some wonderful gift."

We left the restaurant and relived our honeymoon night again and again. In a love drunk stupor, I recall John saying to me, "You need to write me a check more often." It was a night I'll never forget.

Months later, we were out having dinner like we always did once a week. This time it was John who gave me a present after dessert. He placed a delicately wrapped gift box with lace and accented with baby's breathe. I was baffled.

He saw my puzzlement.

"Will you just open it?"

I unwrapped the box, opened it, and inside was an American Express card. "John, I'll never leave home without it!" I said to him jokingly.

"Seriously, why? I thought we were anti-credit cards? Remember all those things you told me about ... ." He cut me off.

"No, No, No. That's not what I said. The truth is you needed to understand how to manage credit cards, and at that time you didn't. You never knew how to use credit cards properly. I am giving you this American Express card because you have proven to me that you are committed to being a recovered credit card-aholic."

We both laughed out loud.

"But seriously, Marilyn, this is the only credit card we will ever have or need."

John went on to explain that with the American Express card, I could purchase something for $1,000 instead of using the $1,000 cash I had in my bank account. The card would allow me to float my money for 30 days, thereby leaving my $1,000 in the bank to earn interest. The terms of the card were as strict as John was about money.

"As soon as the bill comes, Marilyn, you must pay the entire amount off. No monthly payments. No partial payments. No minimum payments - the entire amount must be paid. Can you agree to that?"

"Yes," I said, excited. I felt like a financial equal; the bond of trust growing between us even more.

"Then repeat after me - this is the only credit card we will ever own," he said. I repeated those exact words.

John explained how most couples have unspoken rules about money, and because they are unspoken, there are misunderstandings, mistakes and missteps. The left hand doesn't know what the right is doing, and there's no coordination over the expectations each hand has for the other. Small debts and liabilities grow into larger and larger ones, each partner develops debts expecting that the other partner can help pay off, amplifying the problems.

John believed having one credit card account would alleviate this problem. He knew that every detail of our economic lives needed to be shared. We went home and again revisited our honeymoon night. I fell asleep that night thinking, *"This marriage is going to be awesome. We're going to make a great team. This just might work."*

The American Express card was my first real experience utilizing a credit card the correct way, and sure enough, I got the hang of it. The American Express card and I, developed a good working relationship. I never purchased more on it than I could pay immediately when the bill arrived.

It was a tool – it simplified things, and was a smarter way to manage my money. There were benefits that I had with the card I wouldn't have had with cash. My lesson was that credit cards weren't the enemy, rather financial irresponsibility, financial ignorance and a lack of understanding of my partner's expectations, were the enemy. This enemy was easily defeated.

My marriage to John was happy and we were managing it well. God was the CEO, John was CFO and I was the COO. We were on the same page, had the same mission statement, and united in our vision for a prosperous life together. Every New

Year's Eve, we spent the afternoon charting our plans for the upcoming year – our annual report and prospectus. We'd plan out things like where we would vacation, what home improvements we'd undertake, and whether we were going to buy a new car. John's management skills made him a good head of household. I had developed strong organizing and negotiating skills. We complemented each other well and our partnership remained intact through the remainder of our time in Bismarck, a short stay in Chicago, and a transfer to Houston.

It was in the humid heat of the southwest that credit cards became a steamy issue for us, again. Not knowing how long we would be in Houston, we leased an apartment and lived the lives of gypsies. When we weren't working, we traveled to interesting locales in Texas. We visited cities like Austin, San Antonio, Corpus Christi, and Galveston and popular tourist attractions like the Natural Bridge Caverns. It really was a fun lifestyle. We weren't just husband and wife, we became good friends and developed a wonderful partnership; we were inseparable.

It's amazing how lessons you thought you mastered pop-up again. It came in the form of a shopping trip to a downtown Houston department store. Only ladies can appreciate walking through a store, seeing a drop dead gorgeous dress and developing a "I gotta have it" attack.

There was just one problem, the department store didn't take the American Express card. I had to have that dress! I was quickly losing my right mind. The clerk, who was highly trained in these matters and quite clever, informed me that I could open a charge account and not only have the dress I wanted, but also save 10 percent on my initial purchase. Ten percent! My mind was completely lost at this point. Creditors really try to reel you in with the savings bit. You think they're doing you a favor by saving you money up front. Think again.

I wanted that dress! Still, I knew I had made a bond, a pact set in stone with John. I asked the clerk if she could just hold the dress for me in layaway. They didn't have a layaway plan. My plan was foiled. I knew I could have walked out of that store, but temptation overcame me. I had to have "that" dress.

It was as if my soul had left my body and I was acting on a bad habit many years trammeled. My body acted on it's own with no regard to the desires of my head and heart. All I was thinking about was me in that dress and the 10% discount. That dress visited a forgotten place in my psyche. It kept saying "Buy me now, buy me now, don't wait."

Against better judgment, I got the credit card. I was officially off the wagon. I let a flimsy piece of material - a dress - make me break a promise I made five years earlier to my husband. I quickly put all thoughts and memories of the "crime" I had just committed against my marriage, out of my mind. I was sure I was never going to use that card again. I told myself it was for only one purchase, John will never find out.

I walked out of the store with my fabulous dress and a growing case of selective, voluntary amnesia. The universe hadn't clued me in on the volcano that was about to erupt in my life. I would soon find out that the credit card game is filled with temptations, pitfalls and land mines and I, like a sucker, became a victim.

Some weeks later, I came home from work on a Monday night to find all of my bags packed and stacked at the door. "John, where are we moving to?" I asked with excitement in my voice, sidestepping the luggage and hurrying into the dining room to get the news of our obvious relocating. "Where are we moving to now, New York, Colorado, California, where? You know I've always wanted to live in Los Angeles."

He didn't respond, he had a stern look on his face. The look reminded me of that Saturday afternoon many years ago at a little kitchen table in Chicago. I was chilled and I could feel the goose bumps all over my body. My excitement was immediately halted.

"We are not moving anywhere," said John, "you are moving out - get your stuff and leave."

"Honey, what are you talking about?" My heart was pounding and my palms were sweaty. "What are you saying to me? I don't understand."

"You are a liar, Marilyn." I became even more confused.

"I am not living with a liar."

I had no idea what he was talking about. I just knew that he was serious and I was scared.

"You promised me that you would not stray from our financial commitment to each other. You broke your promise."

"Promise?" I thought and dared not utter. The fog in my mind was not letting up.

"I refuse to be in a marriage with someone who would intentionally sabotage our financial future."

Desperately I tried to understand, "Honey, what are you talking about? I'm not a liar. What did I lie about?" Tears were welling up in my eyes and I was beginning to shake all over. This was one of the worst moments of my life, and I had no idea what financial sin I had committed. I had the creeping, horrifying feeling that I had the day when John said to me **"I can't afford to marry you."**

John leaned back and flipped out a brand new credit card. The card came out of his hand as if in slow motion. When the card hit the table it sounded like a series of explosions as it danced across the table top. It stopped in front of me. Face up. Instantly, the amnesia was gone. It was my new credit card from the department store. My "had to have it dress" suddenly seemed so dispensable.

What had I done?

My marriage was crumbling right before my eyes because of a piece of plastic. This couldn't be happening to me - to us. Was he serious? My husband, recognizing my complete state of confusion and despair, said to me, "Marilyn, we talked about this years ago, and we decided to use only one credit card, the American Express Card. We agreed, didn't we?"

"Yes, baby, but ... ."

"But," he finished my plea, "you're now trying to revert back to your old ways."

"Honey let me explain!" I begged.

"No, you lied to me."

"I know baby, but ... ."

"But nothing. This marriage is over," he said with an ominous finality.

I had broken our financial oath, and a stupid credit card, instant gratification, a silly dress, and me were to blame. I couldn't believe it. Just like that. There was no doubt he meant it.

My devastation had to be put on hold while my survival instincts kicked in. My strategy was to allow time for him to cool off. It was obvious that he had lost all capabilities of clear thought. I needed to wait until he calmed down before I could talk with him. I couldn't believe how I made such a stupid mistake. I was scared. I'd never seen him like this before. The only thing that saved me was Monday Night Football.

I had a couple of things in my favor: he loved football and his favorite team was winning. I knew not to attempt any form of communication until half-time. It seemed like forever, and I was nervously pacing in the kitchen. Finally, when the commercials came on at the end of the first half, I walked into the room, armed with two peace offerings behind my back.

"Honey, can we talk?" If he was surprised that I was still there, he didn't show it.

"No," he said blankly and resolute.

I could tell that the football game had soften him up somewhat. He was stretched out on the sofa. I sat down on the floor in front of him. I handed him the items I had been holding behind my back in quiet ceremony. I placed before him the credit card that had just come in the mail that day, and a pair of scissors.

He looked at the scissors, the credit card, and at me. I could finally see an emotion. I saw disappointment on his face. He sighed heavily, a sigh that gave me hope. John said, "Marilyn, we can't do it your way. And believe me this isn't about my way either. It's all about doing it the right way."

"Honey, I am really, really, really sorry, that I disappointed you. I just made a mistake. Please, you know I am a recovering credit card abuser. I fell off the wagon."

Even though he was trying to hold it back, a little grin slipped through. "Here," I said, handing him the scissors. "You know what you need to do."

He took the scissors and the credit card. As he was cutting it up he asked, "Why didn't you ask me for the money if you didn't have it? You know if there's anything you want that you can't afford, just let me know. I'll give you the money."

Snip, snip. Silently, I watched him reprise his performance from the kitchen table five years earlier as he finished cutting up the credit card into small little pieces. The sound of the scissors disturbed me, but I had done more than break my vow about using credit cards. I was involved in an adulterous relationship with a department store. I had committed financial infidelity. I was a cheater in his eyes.

It wasn't until years later that I discovered that most couples are in serious credit card debt, overextended, and commit financial adultery all the time. Their finances are in utter disarray and teetering on the brink of financial ruin. People underestimate the subversive effects that financial instability has on a relationship. Although not a direct cause, it starts with blaming one another, not talking to one another, and not making love to one another. Eventually, the marriage killers begin to add up.

I was so relieved. Finally, with total conviction, I promised my husband I would never be financially disloyal again. And I never did. My marriage was more important to me than a quick mental high from a new purchase. It was just a dress; nothing wears as well as financial harmony in a marriage feels.

Logan's Lessons

There would be no "The love of money is the root of all evil," if there were no temptations of what money can buy. Even in the most well managed relationships, we sometimes get wayward and fall from financial grace.

My advice is:

- Recognize your temptation triggers and develop strategies to avoid them.

- Remember, financial infidelity is the number one cause for divorce.

- Don't allow money and credit cards to be a proxy for something it isn't - love, acceptance, self-esteem and power.

- Review your financial goals at least every four months.

- Remember, there is no want greater than your want for a successful marriage.

CHAPTER 5

Put Stock In Your Marriage

I have to confess that during our marriage I turned into - are you ready for this? — a "wife." The truth is, I was extremely happy about the fact. I loved this man so much. I remember writing my mother-in-law thanking her for raising a wonderful son who turned out to be a fabulous husband, my husband. He was really caring and I always felt as if he loved me more than I loved myself.

John and I decided to stay in Houston. I was beginning to wear the hat of "wife" well.

John took to the traditional role of "husband." He took the responsibilities he believed went with that role quite seriously. I was a career woman. My job was to work - if I chose to, keep the house in order, and spend my money on me. His job was to work, take care of all our financial needs, empty the trash, pay for the vacations, and spend his money on me; all John's design. I was the June to his Ward, sans Wally and The Beaver.

We had two cars, which John maintained. Whichever car was filled with gas, was mine for the day. I would ask John which car to drive and he would direct me to the one with gas in it without giving it a thought.

Now, I know what you're thinking about me right about now, but wait a minute. He benefited in more ways than one. And don't forget - this was his suggested financial arrangement.

Our marriage worked for both of us. It wasn't until my girl-friends and I started a group for married couples called "**What Makes Yours (marriage) Work?**" that I found out that our marriage worked quite differently than others.

The club rules we set up were simple. The hosts had to choose the topic of conversation. Spouses had to sit next to each other, always with hands held. We thought if you had intimate contact with your spouse this would reduce anger; there was a lot of hand holding that came undone. Each couple was limited to five minutes to present their views on the topic, which kept the gatherings moving in a timely manner and allowed every couple to have input.

The meetings were usually fun and full of non-stop laughter. The topics ranged from sex, raising children (we had little to say about that), dealing with relatives, to career goals. The one topic that was most volatile was the subject of money. Money proved to be the butterfly that spawned the storm; the more each couple talked, the more the intensity of the conversation grew. He would blame her for charging too much on their credit cards. She would blame him for spending too much money on his hobbies, golf, computer gadgets, and hanging out with his buddies. Couples would point the finger with acrimony and a zealots fervor. The power struggle and control issues were at the core of the bickering.

It was evident that our friends were not in synch with their financial goals. The resentment was thick and it underscored for me that the misuse of money is a cancer that kills marriages. John and I would quietly sit in amazement, because we simply assumed that our friends managed their finances as we did. We thought because there were so many similarities between us as couples that they managed their money issues with little conflict. We took for granted that we were alike; were we wrong.

Through these conversations I discovered these couples were splitting mortgages and utility bills in half: his half and her half. When it came to vacations, each spouse got his or her transportation reservations paid any way they saw fit. "Just charge it" was a popular philosophy. The hotel expenses were divided also. I couldn't believe my ears; no one was on the same page. More times than not, they were both spending borrowed money. When the time would come for John and I to share our financial arrangement, all I could think was, "Oh my goodness, John might consider their style of 'financial room-mating' for us."

John spoke first. He proceeded to tell everyone that in our home, he took care of everything.

"Everything?" all asked in unison. The women stared at me and the men sat there shaking their heads. They all wanted to know what bills I was responsible for and what I did with the money I made. I simply let them know that John and I had found a system that worked for us. We decided early on that we were not going to allow money – or the management of it – to divide us. I let them know that John helped me realize that I had a spending problem, and he helped me understand the importance of credit. Our friends looked at us as if they were seeing us, or something like us, for the first time; as if we were extraterrestrials.

Our agreement had evolved. It was a business plan open to revision as needed and as agreed upon. It wasn't like I didn't want to contribute more financially to the marriage. The first two weeks after the wedding, John and I had debated about this very issue. After all, I was accustomed to supporting myself. Why wouldn't I expect to be a financial partner post-wedding?

"No, Marilyn," John would counter whenever the subject came up. "I am your husband and my job is to provide for you."

No one ever explained to me what it took for a man to be a husband. I grew up in a household with a divorced mom who struggled to make ends meet on public assistance. I didn't have any knowledge of what a husband's role was, particularly with reference to money. It took me a while to understand that in John's mind, there were certain things he needed to do in order to believe he was functioning properly as a husband. So, I allowed him to be the man and the type of husband that made him feel whole, responsible and caring.

Still, my conscience would not allow me to settle on no financial contribution. One day, during a heated debate, I told John I felt like a "kept woman." He relented and agreed to two responsibilities for me. First of all, I would pay the phone bill. Not much of a sacrifice, I reminded him, since I was the only one who really used the phone. John just looked at me with those dark brown eyes. After giving it a moment or two of thought, I could tell he had found something else, "Okay, then *you* can also buy the groceries."

This was a task I could literally put my teeth into. However, I hadn't spent money on groceries once I began munching off my relatives. After I took on the responsibility as Head of Grocery Procurement for Logan Corp, I was taken aback by how much food cost. I grew up poor, so every penny counted and was recounted. My mother always knew exactly how much we had to spend on groceries. When I was single, I spent money looking like the Joneses not eating like them. I couldn't afford to buy groceries. Yet, when I was living with my mother, we always shopped from a very detailed list, always had a strict budget and bought generic.

John, although he was very frugal with his money, had a philosophy of never compromising on food – buy the best products. When he'd go grocery shopping, he would just grab the basket go up and down the aisles and buy whatever he wanted with wild abandon.

To give John the quality food he wanted, yet stay within our budget, I used my mother's budgeting skills coupled with my coupon saving savvy when buying groceries. As long as I was not accruing debt, John and I were happy. We were happy watching our savings grow. He literally provided for everything, but my contributions were keeping our household costs down.

Meal planning always reduced my costs. I maintained a calendar that tracked what I would cook for a month, which helped me plan purchases. On Sundays, I cooked enough dinner for five days. Five plates for John and five plates for me were stored in the refrigerator, his on the left side and mine on the right. (Don't ask for seconds at my home unless you want to eat tomorrow's dinner.)

When I tried to defend my grocery shopping as a valuable contribution to our family, one of the women in the group announced that she had gone shopping with me and knew how little I really spent on groceries. I couldn't put my hands over John's ears fast enough to prevent him from hearing these troubling remarks.

"Marilyn, how much money do you make a year?" asked one man. "So when you get paid, you only buy food?" he continued. The inquiries and comments kept coming. The subject of wills and estate planning was brought up next to which John responded that we already had a plan in place, which set-off another round of blank stares and open mouths. None of the other couples had prepared for death. I glanced at John from time to time to see how he was responding to all of the negative attention I thought we were receiving. The look on his face began to change, as if he was thinking that maybe our friends were right.

"They are not right!" I screamed in my mind. *"Stop listening to them."* Well, they might have been correct when we first got married, when I wanted to contribute equally. Nevertheless, I had gotten used to our arrangement. I wasn't going to let them interrupt our financial bond. Eventually there was nothing else to be

said. We moved on to the next couple, but only after the wives let me know I had it made and the husbands let it be known that they wanted to be me.

The ride home from the marriage group meeting was quiet. John and I usually would discuss the high points of the evening and the couple that stood out. It never failed, no matter the topic, it always seemed to focus on one couple. This time, we were that couple. I pretended to be too sleepy to talk and we drove home in silence.

To my relief and delight, after a brief discussion the next morning, John and I agreed that we would keep our financial system in place; it worked for us. My grandmother would always say "Love many, trust few, always paddle your own canoe." It definitely applied here.

Both products of broken homes, John and I realized early on that we didn't want to end up divorced like our parents. We made room for each other's differences and strengths. John's tendencies were more conservative and mine were more adventurous. We were able to blend them both to achieve harmony. Despite our earlier credit card episodes, we found a way to have stability with our finances.

John and I learned to navigate our own financial dynamics. He spent money on our needs and wants with no questions asked. I purchased my wants, bargaining all the way to the final sale. Still, we were both generally conservative spenders. We were determined to live within our means and not allow money to become a proxy for something it wasn't – power or love. As the risk taker, I was always throwing ideas out to John on how we could make our money work for us. Hidden inside me was the spirit of an entrepreneur. I would always come up with money-making ventures that John would allow me to explore. Once I had a hotdog stand at a festival. I bought 5,000 hotdogs, but only sold 250. This was the type of dog that bit me in my butt, and John reluctantly became a lover of hotdog casserole and hotdog pie. You'd be surprised the number of fun uses you can find for hot dogs.

The money risks, however, paid off in lessons learned or in unexpected gains. Occasionally, my risk taking paid off for us. I worked in a downtown Houston law firm, where I spent most of my time at a computer. One day, during a lull in work, I began thinking about how computers had changed everyday living; from my first job as a clerk to now as a paralegal my job was easier because of computers. Paperwork wasn't an issue; information was stored much easier and made the interoffice mail guy obsolete. I was quickly realizing that computers could potentially replace me. This line of thinking made me ponder what computers could not replace. It was a little mental exercise for me. In the middle of this exercise, John called. We chatted for a few moments and made plans for the evening. After we hung up, it hit me: "SEX," I screamed out. *Computers could not replace sex!*

People would always have sex, if for no other reason than to create life. There was another reason sex was necessary, one that in my mind men had invented - extra-marital affairs. Women were entering the workforce in huge numbers. It was only a matter of time before there would be more work-related affairs initiated by women. If women were going to partake in the game,

I reasoned, they would be smarter about keeping affairs discrete. Their indiscretion would not be exposed by unplanned children and diseases.

I arrived at the conclusion that women would increase condom sales. They would be wiser shoppers and would purchase condoms in bulk, instead of individually. Taking all of that into consideration, I decided to invest in the condom industry. It would be a move that would take our family's nest egg beyond John's employer's stock and stock options.

I picked up the phone and called the drugstore close to our home. "I have a weird question. Can you go to the shelf and give me the names of your condoms and the companies that make them?" Without hesitation, the clerk on the other end of the receiver rattled off several of their top suppliers. Armed with five company names, I quickly discovered that one brand was publicly traded. It was a British company that was traded as a penny stock, which meant that it sold for under $1.00. Not knowing how to work with a stockbroker or wanting to alert John, I called a friend I presumed had some market savvy.

When I shared my idea of a condom stock purchase, he said, "Marilyn, you know nothing about the stock market. You will probably lose all of your money. Why not leave this to the professionals?"

After those negative comments, I chose to be more careful with whom I shared my new stock purchase financial plan. I would not be deterred. My idea made too much sense to me and I became bullheaded. The public library became my stock research heaven. The stock was selling at 42 cents a share. After about a month, the stock reached 50 cents a share. I contacted a brokerage firm and was assigned a stockbroker. I instructed him to purchase for me 5000 shares and didn't tell a soul.

The credit card fiasco was the first finance related secret I kept from John; this would be my second. The subject of investing in stocks was never discussed, so I was not breaking any of our financial rules. I felt like I was on solid ground. This was my money, and I wasn't incurring debt. This couldn't be considered financial infidelity.

Months later, the stock reached $3 a share. The stockbroker and I became avid watchers of this condom market. He eventually advised some of his clients to invest. He would convince them by sharing my reasoning, but he would get all the credit. He considered me his undercover stock picker.

When the stock hit $4.50 a share, I decided it was time to reveal my secret to John. I prepared his favorite meal to soften him up before I served up my secret. He had no reason to be suspicious until I told him, "We have to talk."

As if he were Ricky Ricardo, he asked me, "What have you done now?"

I began, "Well, this stock ... ." I

"Stock?" John interrupted, his body tensing slightly. "... That I bought," I continued.

"That you bought?" he asked, struggling to keep his cool. "What?!" He lost the struggle.

I spoke with the speed of an auctioneer, not allowing him to interject any negative comments. "I bought this stock at 50 cents a share and now it's trading at $4.50 a share."

"How much did you buy?" he asked.

"I bought 5000 shares," I announced. The tension in the room did an about-face.

"Why didn't you buy more?" he asked in a tone signaling that he was proud of my decision.

Afterwards, I told family, friends, and strangers, that they should invest in condoms. My gift giving items for birthdays, Christmas, and other special occasions, were the brand of condoms I owned stock in. I figured folks were going to have sex anyway, so they might as well use my condoms. As far as I was concerned, I was the owner of a McDonald's franchise, so shouldn't my friends buy a burger from me every once in a while?

By the time I sold the stock, it had reached $39 a share, and AIDS had become an epidemic. For a long time, among family and friends, I was commonly referred to as the Condom Queen.

Logan's Lessons

Good sound financial management and planning allow for calculated risks to be taken. Because we were in a good financial situation, I was able to take on the investment risk. However, be reminded that all risks do not necessarily lead to a positive outcome.

My advice is:

- Only risk money you can lose without changing your lifestyle.

- Be wise with investments – do your homework.

- Wealth comes from disciplined saving. You should be saving 15% of your after tax dollars.

- Join an investment club or start one of your own.

- ALWAYS put the maximum allowed into your retirement account and/or 401k. ALWAYS!

CHAPTER 6

Hope For The Best, Plan For The Worst

My tendency to look ahead and ask "What if?" had been with me from a young age, and it didn't occur to me to curb it after I married. Even though our marriage seemed solid and it was the envy of many of our wedded and unwedded friends, I wasn't unprepared for the worst-case scenario. Although it was a good marriage, I wasn't immune from insecurity. I was always poised for the other shoe to drop.

Given our divorced parents' backgrounds, I knew there was always a chance it would not last forever. Just in case, I always maintained a separate savings account with enough money to pay for an apartment, a car or other expenses. I was no dummy. I wasn't going to be stranded without a roof over my head, and a way to get to a job. I saw how much of a struggle it was for my mother when my father left. There were no obvious marriage busters brewing between John and I, but I always wanted to be prepared. Regardless of the sentiment, even the most detached husband wouldn't feel good about his wife having a secret account. John never found out about it.

We enjoyed spoiling one another with little surprises and taking exotic vacations to romantic locations, such as Cozumel, the Virgin Islands, and Aruba. I brought out the playful boy in him, and he brought out the sophisticated woman in me. Our lives were filled with laughter, excitement, joy, and overall peace.

After eight years of marriage, we were physically, mentally and financially prepared to become parents. We were both born in August and wanted our children to share our birth month, but as Mother Nature would have it, John Wesley, III, (Trey) was born in July. His arrival made the picture more perfect. I distinctly remember a day when John and I stood in the doorway to our backyard and watched our 1-year-old son playing in his sandbox. It was one of those indescribable moments filled with pure joy.

I felt content; our relationship and family were truly at peace. With my eyes on Trey, I said to John, "We only have two important things to do in life."

"Really?" he said. "What are those?"

"Number one, to raise Trey and Number two to die," I said. "Those are the two pivotal issues that we have to face in life. We have a wonderful marriage, great careers, and a beautiful life. We have traveled, acquired nice homes, cars, developed great friendships, and in the process we have become best friends. We are living a life most people dream about."

John approached his job with an incredibly strong work ethic. He wasn't a workaholic, but he believed in doing whatever it took to do the job right. His favorite saying was, "If a job has once begun, never leave it until it's done; whether the task is great or small do it well or not at all." You would always find him reciting this to his colleagues at work. A month after Trey's first birthday, he began working long hours, seven days a week; 12 to 15 hours a day.

He worked as chief project manager for an oil refinery. It was essentially an office job, but John always felt it was occasionally important to get in "with the troops." Every year the company would have what is called a "turnaround" where they shut part of the refinery down for maintenance.

One night, John came home, as usual, just in time for dinner. We were in bed by 10 and had just fallen asleep in each other's arms when the phone rang. It was a shift manager with the news that something had gone wrong at the plant. The company was going to potentially lose millions of dollars a day if the problem was not quickly corrected. When John hung up the phone, he went to his closet and began to get dressed.

I asked him where he was going. He told me about the problem at the refinery and that he needed to be there. John climbed the corporate ladder at rapid pace and deservedly so. He was considered one of the brightest executives in the nation. I thought to myself, *Why couldn't he call someone else's husband, and have them fix the problem?*

Why couldn't he send some subordinate who needed to impress management? Even though he was part of management,

John never thought he was above the "impress-me stage." Sensing the urgency of the matter, John knew what he had to do.

"John," I said. "You don't have to work this hard anymore."

He looked at me and said, "No, Marilyn, you don't understand. I still have to go beyond the call of duty. I don't have the luxury of my counterparts. This is something I have to do."

I was upset. I knew he was right, and I knew he was a company man who would go when he was called. I heard the garage door go up. It wasn't like John to leave without giving me a kiss. Throughout our whole marriage, John always made it a habit of kissing me good-bye whenever he left home. It's one of those wonderful, treasured moments of connection; a way of knowing each other by the habits you keep. His friends often teased him about it. I just thought it was the way things were supposed to be. A few minutes went by and I didn't hear the car start or the garage door go down. John crept back into our bedroom and gave me a kiss. I then heard the door to Trey's room open. John must have given Trey a kiss, too. Then, he left.

I fell back to sleep. I distinctly remember the phone ringing at 11:30 p.m., I just thought it was John calling, letting me know what time he would be home. I knew something was wrong when I didn't recognize the voice on the other end, it was a man's measured and monotone voice and he simply said, "Mrs. Logan, there's been an accident."

"Is he okay?" was all I asked. "Well, there has been an explosion at the refinery and John has been injured. He's at Galveston's John Sealy Hospital. Can you get there?"

"Yes."

"Are you going to get somebody ... ?"

I cut him off and replied, "Don't worry. I will get there."

A sense of measured urgency came over me; it was if I had practiced for this day and now practice was paying off. I threw on some clothes with the speed of a firefighter and went down the hall to tell my younger sister Michelle, who had come from Chicago to visit, that I had to leave. I didn't share any other information, probably because I wanted to concentrate on praying for the best and sparing her the worst. I called my next-door neighbor, Aaron, and asked him to drive me to the hospital.

Aaron had served in the military as a corps medic and he knew this particular hospital specialized in trauma care. He tried to prepare me. He told me that John could have been flown to the medical center in Houston, but there must have been a reason they took him to Galveston instead.

We arrived at the hospital to the chaos of white coats and clipboards. Aaron had to leave and in his absence, I realized that I was alone with no one to hold me and convince me that all would be well. The very person that did that for me was somewhere in this sterile maze of beeps and squawks. I needed to tell somebody what was going on. It was now 1:00 a.m. and I was the only one in my family with the bad news.

I called my mother back in Chicago. My cool demeanor was quickly replaced by incoherent babbling and sobs at the sound of my mother's voice. My mind was spinning trying to calculate every horrible possibility. I tried to express every thought as it came to me, but my mouth could not keep the same frenetic pace. My mother was patient with me and was finally able to coax me to slow down. When she could finally make some sense of what I was saying, she began asking questions I could not yet answer. She promised to call John's mother and I began calling John's friends, many of whom went to college with him at Purdue University.

By the time the sun started rising, I wasn't alone anymore. There were about 20 other family members and friends around. I quickly learned something about myself. When something bad is going on, I don't want an audience. The more people came, the more places I tried to find to hide. I just wanted to see John. The doctors were evasive and kept me at bay, saying there were procedures that needed to be performed. Five hours had passed since I arrived at the hospital and I still had not seen John, and had no clue about his condition. I knew he was in critical condition; otherwise they would have allowed me to see him.

I was told that they would have to perform surgery. The *accident happened* at 11:10 p.m., and he was scheduled for surgery at 7:00 a.m. the next morning. I thought to myself, *"He's not going to make it. Why are they waiting so long to operate? Seven a.m. is hours from now!"* In the midst of disarray, a person's mind can still focus. I began to think, *If they could save him, they would have performed surgery immediately. There must be a serious problem.*

John's surgery began two hours later than scheduled at 9:00 a.m. Late that afternoon he was placed into intensive care and I saw John for the very first time. The doctor attempted to explain John's situation. I was looking at him intently trying to get a read, but I didn't hear a word he said. The situation was all too surreal now that I could see John. Time bent and twisted. I was in a fog. Nothing was real. I did not know what to expect. John was laying there inert with his head wrapped in a turban of gauze and tape. His face was motionless and still beautiful, but different. His radiance was gone. I felt instantly that the spirit of the man I loved was no more. I clung dearly to hope; John's life and my sanity depended on it.

In a brief spell of clarity I was finally able to comprehend what the doctor had been trying to tell me. The doctor told me that John had sustained a massive head injury and that he was in a coma, but he didn't give me a prognosis. I was determined that everything would be okay. I would make it so. I would will it so, and even pray it so. John was going to survive. I was dealing with the horror of what was happening by diverting my thoughts to thinking about how I would care for John.

It was almost reassuring to think that I would be forced to sell our home so that we could move closer to a rehab center; it meant John would still be with me. I wondered what kind of nurse we would have to hire, when would they release him from the hospital, and how long it would take before our lives would have some sense of normalcy.

The emotional intensity of seeing John lying there still became too much. I could no longer process the thoughts of sadness, helplessness, and uncertainty. My emotions shut down. I could no longer cry. My sobs were quieted. I could only look at John. I sat there - still. John's situation was touch-and-go. I got a hotel room nearby, and my friend, Kathy agreed to stay with me. It was now Thursday; just a few nights after the accident. I was drifting in and out of sleep caught in that place between reality and dreams. In this altered consciousness, I had a prophetic vision about a funeral, John's funeral. I awoke knowing there was something I had to do. My eyes flew open and on the television in front of me, was a man dressed in a black robe, who was singing gospel in a beautiful deep voice that touched the root of my soul.

I looked over at Kathy and said, "I've got to get that man to sing at the funeral."

Kathy was clearly concerned about me. "Marilyn, John is not going to die," she said. "You know he is going to make it, don't you? You're not making any sense."

I appreciated her wishful thinking, however, the dream was subconsciously revealing my reality. I told her about it; how everyone was dressed in beautiful bright clothes and that the man whom we had just seen on television sang at the funeral service. I told her that John wasn't coming home. We were a fun couple, who loved to entertain. John was going to stay alive long enough for me to arrange his funeral in the way he would want it.

While everyone else talked about John's recovery, I spoke to the people who could help me determine my next steps. I pulled the doctors aside and asked them if I needed to plan a funeral. "Yes, Mrs. Logan," they said. It was as if they were relieved to know that I wanted the truth. To verify their remarks, I questioned a neighbor friend who worked at the hospital and knew about the accident. She too responded, "Marilyn, he is not coming home." I left the hospital and all my family and friends that very night.

Logan's Lessons

If you live long enough, life will test you. The top four reasons for financial instability are loss of job, death, sickness and divorce. Lifestyle change can occur quickly; always be prepared for the "what if?" There are specific things individuals and couples should have in place.

My advice is:

- Review life and disability policies annually.

- Make certain that you have a Living Will and a Will or Trust.

- In a two income household, the goal should be to live off one income and save the other.

- Always keep a "just-in-case" account.

CHAPTER 7

When It Rains, It Pours

It was odd to go back to the house that John and I shared knowing he would never be there again. I purchased an over-the-counter sleep aid and for the first few days, it was just that drug and me. It helped me sleep, but it also helped me deal with the constant phone calls from the friends and family who were still at the hospital cheering John on. They didn't understand why I was no longer holding vigil at the hospital.

During a moment of clarity, I realized that I wanted to have more children by John. Hospital officials told me that they had never taken sperm from someone who couldn't sign the permission request. This was an ordeal in and of itself. The hospital's representatives thought I had lost my mind. They had to confer with their attorney, which took a couple of days. Then I had to undergo psychiatric evaluations with three different physicians.

Why not just deal with the situation, remarry and have more children, they asked. I responded that if technology was going to allow me to use my husband's sperm in a bank for my future use, I wanted to utilize it. My request was finally approved.

I couldn't be the broken down crazed wife everyone wanted me to be; not now at least, it was not in my nature I was a survivor. Ten days had gone by since John's accident and I was worn out, but I still had funerals to arrange - one for Houston and one for Chicago, where John would be buried. Two of my girlfriends promised to help me once I finally convinced them that John would not be coming home.

It was a first for all of us and it showed. When the man at the funeral home told me I had to pick out a casket, I asked for a casket catalogue. "A catalogue?" the man asked, his manner heavy with sympathetic patience. "You will have to go into the room where we keep our models and pick one out." My friends looked at me as if to say, "Girl, you're on your own."

I was not going to make this choice alone. I locked arms with them and stood at the doorway of the room housing the caskets. A female employee opened the door for us and we peeked in. I pointed to the casket closest to the door. "That one right there," I said quickly. "Don't you want to look at all of our selection?" she asked. We found the courage to go in and look at the rest of the coffins and I chose a beautiful, blue, top-of-the-line casket for John.

With the Houston arrangements made, I contacted a friend in Chicago to help me with the Chicago arrangements. People began to get wind of my plans and my phone rang almost non-stop. No one wanted me to accept that it is was the end for John. They all encouraged me to pray. I listened patiently. I knew what I had to do and I was not going to be dissuaded. I'm certain they meant well, but some crisis require action, not words. The callers had yet to accept John's fate and I didn't have time to convince them otherwise. I was moving on.

Ironically, I was in a hospital in Houston when I got the call that I had been expecting from the hospital in Galveston. A couple of days earlier, Trey had fallen off of his scooter and hit his head. I raced out of the house with him in my arms, leaving my contacts and eyeglasses behind. I headed towards the Houston medical center, 35 miles away.

I could barely see three feet ahead of me, but with God's grace we made it to the hospital safely. My baby and I both looked rough. I was frazzled and disheveled and my clothes did not say otherwise. I'm sure they thought I was a drug addict or homeless. Trey only had a t-shirt and a diaper on. The nurses listened to my story, started treatment on my son, and called the police with a suspicion of child neglect.

After the police called the hospital in Galveston, they believed my story about Trey's scooter. The doctor told me I could take him home, but if he developed a fever to bring him back.

Sure enough, Trey developed that fever and I was back at the hospital in less than 24 hours. When we arrived at the hospital, my appearance had further declined. There had not been enough time from my first visit for the hospital to file Trey's medical records, so the police were called in, again. At some point during this second go around, I blacked out.

I woke up in a bed next to a crib where Trey was sleeping. A number of tubes were connected to his small body. It was about four in the morning and the hospital was quiet. It took a while to get the plaque off of my mind before the reality of the situation became lucid.

For the first time in days, there were no companions, drugs, or emergencies to distract me from me. Many questions crowded my mind, but there was one that kept rising to the top - how had my life seemingly collapsed so quickly? Two weeks ago I had a great husband, healthy toddler and not a worry in sight. While my husband sat in a coma in another hospital. I kept coming up short with answers. For the first time in years, I thought, "I want my mommy to fix this." I just wanted the problems to be taken away.

My pity party was interrupted by the phone ringing. It startled me and started my heart pounding. I picked up the receiver, thinking it was the wrong number.

"Mrs. Logan?" the voice asked.

"Yes," I answered.

"We tracked you down to this number. We wanted to let you know that your husband, John, has died."

In all of my "what-if" scenarios, played over and over in my mind before the accident about our marriage, I never really envisioned losing John to death. I thought about losing him to another woman or even divorce, but never death. Unfortunately, someday, in some way, everything must come to an end.

I truly did believe "for better or for worse, for richer for poorer, in sickness and in health, until death do us part." I meant that when I said it, and I'm sure John meant it too. I just wasn't ready to accept the consequences. Not then, not now, not ever.

An industrial accident at an oil refinery had spared three people and taken one, my husband, from me and my son. I couldn't find any answers. There was no peace or conscience for the way that John died.

My anger with God had now grown to a size that I could no longer contain. I threw questions at Him: why do you hate me so? Why did you take my perfect life and turn it upside down? Why did you take the most important person from me?

God has a way of answering back. In the depths of my anger I heard a voice that said, "Stop being so ungrateful and focus on the precious gift that he has given you. I want you to look at the life that I have given you, the years you had to share with this man, your beautiful son, and all that you have learned from the relationship."

A familiar calm suddenly filled me. I knew that Trey was going to be okay. I looked over at him and I said, "God, thanks for giving me John to love and Trey to raise. I'm not mad at you anymore."

John had waited for me. The final details of his Houston funeral had been completed two days before he died. Relatives began to flood to our home; they all wanted to help out. There were enough good intentions to pave a very long road.

The funeral service was beautiful, complete with the singing of Hanq Neal, the singer from my dream and who I had seen on television. He wowed us with a soul-stirring rendition of "Ordinary People." The reception that followed was like the parties John and I had given at our home. People apologized for having so much fun. I reassured them that was exactly how we wanted them to feel and how I wanted them to say good-bye to John. After the funeral, I went away for a couple of weeks. I had to get away from everything and everybody and come to terms with the fact that the rest of my life would be without John. The present and the future were pulling at me and I had to face them both. As it turned out, the next phase of my life would teach me more than I could have ever dreamed about life, finances, and myself.

Logan's Lessons

Damn, I miss you John.

CHAPTER 8

You Can Do Better Than That

Chicago was where I was born and grew up, but Houston was the home John and I had built together. Over the loving objections of my family who wanted me to return to my roots in Chicago, Trey and I boarded a plane and headed back to Houston after our time away. It was our home. It was where we belonged.

Although everything was as we left it, nothing was the same. I didn't know where to start. Reminders that I was the remaining half of a once vibrant couple came one right after the other: John's empty spot in the bed, the lingering scent of his aftershave in his clothes, and his favorite meals no longer prepared. I'd wake up at night reaching for him. I'd hear a car pull into a nearby drive and just for a moment forget he wasn't coming home again.

I'd catch myself in mid-sentence when correcting Trey, "Don't that's your fath... ."

The little occurrences of everyday living that most people take - that I once took, for granted became larger-than-life issues for me. My frustrations and isolation exacerbated the smallest annoyances; mole hills became mountains, ponds became oceans, almost everything began to seem insurmountable.

I was so frazzled. One night I found myself furious with the local gas station. I was certain that their gas tank nozzle was broken. I was trying to put gas in my car and the nozzle wouldn't fit. There was a little speaker box with a sign that read "Press for Assistance." I pressed the button and spoke in a loud and staccato, "It's - broken! Could you come - out - and - fix - it?"

The attendant came out, took one look and said, "Ma'am, you are trying to put leaded gas in an unleaded car."

I became indignant.

"How do _you_ know which gas this car needs, sir?" It was, after all, my car.

He glanced at the car and said matter-of-factly, "It's right here on the door." As he started to walk away he pointed a greasy black stained finger right at the little label that says, "Unleaded Fuel Only" and gave me a toothy grin I've never forgotten.

I stood there crying a river of tears. I felt so incompetent. I was thinking, _"Oh, my God, I don't even know which type of gas belongs in this car."_ The only thing I knew for sure was that I didn't want to feel this way, and I didn't want to have the gas spilling on my hands anymore, and I didn't want to feel overwhelmed. I just wanted things back the way they had been before the nightmare began.

Then the garage door broke. I called Sears to replace it with a new door and they sent out a contractor to install it. I came home that night and pressed the garage door opener like I had done for years. Miraculously the door opened all right, but the light did not come on! I was furious and upset. I couldn't wait to call Sears and rip them to pieces. When the service department came on the line, I screamed into the phone, "Sears, get over here now! My garage door isn't working! Do you people know what you are doing?! The light does not even come on."

The guy on the other end of the phone, God bless him, said, "Ma'am, calm down. Did you put a light bulb in it?"

I just stood there mouth wide open with no clue of what to say. I thought, *"Light bulb? I never knew the garage door opener operated with a light bulb!"* Really, I didn't know that. I just thought, *Hit a switch, the door comes up, and the light comes on, right?* I allowed myself to become so dependent on John that I had ignored such a small detail.

I didn't know the first thing about our bills, our money, or our finances. Suddenly, it seemed that my contribution to the marriage was unimportant and insignificant. John had made attempts to educate me about finances, but ignorance felt so good. I would say, "Honey, I don't want to know about that. You do it. Just let me know when you need my signature."

I was now lost and overwhelmed. My marriage to John had kept me loved, protected, and constantly cared for, but my indifference left me unable to handle the larger financial world on my own. I was beginning to feel resentful, but most of all I was scared. I could grocery shop with the best, but the mortgage company didn't have triple coupon days. Anger, grief, resentment, isolation – that's a poisonous cocktail in the best times of your life. Here, at the nadir of my life's arc, it was a hemlock that nearly left me unswayably depressed.

The thing about feeling like you have lost everything is, you no longer have anything to lose. You can either give up or start again. I'm not a quitter. My son needed someone he could depend on even more than I did. I had no other alternative than to face my fears. I had at least one resource - my life before John Wesley Logan, Jr.

Before I got married, I had a full-time job and attended college. I maintained my own apartment and car, alone. I had been self-sufficient once before, I was going to have to learn to be self-sufficient again, for my son and for me.

I closed myself up in a room trying to make sense of stacks of paperwork. I didn't know who to pay our mortgage to or how the interest rate affected the payment - much less the rate of interest. I was unaware of the utility expenses or who to pay for the landscaping. I only knew two things, how to buy food and how to pay the phone bill.

It was beginning to dawn on me that I was going to have to face the fact that I was a widow with a young child to support. No one had given me any training for this. I didn't have the luxuries of books like "How to Succeed as a Widow" or "The Idiot's Guide to Being a Widow." I had to take care of my son. I had to take care of me. I had to learn about living life as a widow, raising a child alone, life itself, and how to be the financial head of the house. It turned out I had a lot to learn. The memories of John and the responsibilities of my new life were nearly overwhelming. I had to focus on the future, not the past.

I had to start anew in a way that I could manage. I decided to make a move, literally. I packed up my things and closed the door to the master bedroom that we had shared and moved to a smaller bedroom downstairs. It was a significant step that took all the strength I could muster. Changing bedrooms was not going to change my life. It was time to take a bigger and more difficult step. With a great deal of anxiety and apprehension, I decided to sell our home.

Selling the house meant coming to terms with the things John had left behind. It had been over a year, and I had never opened his chest of drawers or the closet that held his clothes. When I got the courage to do it, the smell of John broke through the stale air and all of the memories came rushing back.

As I sorted his things into piles, either for use by friends or to give away, I refused help from anyone. I wanted my hands to touch every sock, t-shirt, suit, and tie. I told him good-bye with every piece I held. I must have said good-bye at least a thousand times.

It was extremely painful and I did more than my share of crying, but it was cheaper than going to therapy. Maybe it took me a year to get to the acceptance stage, and maybe that's what helped me finally push through it. The task was one of the most bittersweet memories I hold to after John was taken from us, and I wouldn't trade that for anything.

The house sold quickly. With Trey's little hand in mine, I was closing one chapter in our lives and opening another one with no clue about what lay ahead. The sale of our home was the first major financial hurdle. The entire process was complicated and confusing. I never let on that I didn't understand any of the logistics.

I sat in my chair looking extremely intelligent, my pen poised confidently. Sign here, initial there. I signed with the confidence of a veteran. Initial here, here and here. The pen danced in my hand like it was part of my body. Sign here, initial here and here, and sign here, sign here, date it and we're done. I had absolutely no clue what I was doing. I was too embarrassed to ask anyone to stop and explain. I had that same feeling I had when I purchased my first car – another easy sale at my expense.

That was my first mistake. It does no good to play smart if you're ignorant – it just makes you look like a fool who is happy to be taken advantage of. If someone had really explained to me what I was doing, I would have learned that I was making a financial blunder. I should have never sold that house. John and I had made a large down payment, signed a 15-year mortgage, and only 12 years remained to repay the loan. If I had been educated in real estate, I would have rented the house and used the excess income to pay for my new home. Better to be a wooly ignorant sheep in winter than a smart fleeced one.

Odds are I would not have listened anyway. I had no confidence in what I was doing in general, much less in owning and maintaining property. I hired an accountant to handle my finances. He tried to get me more involved, but ignorance felt so good. Here I was making the same mistake again. I became a renter and agreed to give my money to a landlord. I didn't want to deal with the responsibilities of caring for a house. What a great idea. Freedom from landscaping and maintenance, in exchange for servitude to a landlord.

It takes time for all of us to adjust to a life crisis; for some people it takes longer than others. The Chinese word for "problem" and "opportunity" are one and the same. The lessons you have to learn are never easy and the path is filled with potholes, broken signs and bandits lying in wait.

It was a year after John's death that I finally took my wedding ring off. It just seemed like the right time. There was no budding relationship driving the decision although there were men who expressed interest. One lived in Chicago, however, the long distance prevented anything from getting serious, he was someone I could talk to and lean on.

It was a business venture that led to the man I would let into my life longer than anyone since my husband's death. We met at a meeting where he was part of a team looking for investors to fund a project. I was drawn to the project and eventually to him. He was the opposite of John. In truth, he wasn't even in John's league. I couldn't pass up the adventure of being the woman who could change a man and smooth out his rough edges.

Within a month of dating him, I realized I was making a tragic mistake. He was jealous of my life and my friends and showed his rancor with verbal abuse. I tried to help him out of his place of self-loathing and jealousy by being a model of poise and patience under duress. He responded with manipulation.

I bought him expensive clothes and gave him the use of my car. He took full advantage. I knew I was in trouble when I had to call a cab to go to the grocery store or to pick up my son from school because my "friend" was gone somewhere leaving me without transportation. The relationship was spiraling downward with no hope in sight, but I attempted to keep it alive. It didn't and still doesn't make sense, but I felt "half a man is better than no man."

My efforts were rewarded with physical abuse. The first time it happened in front of one of his friends. I didn't get the hint. Another time it happened as I was on my way to my car with my son. Though he tried to beat me to death, we got away. The thought of getting away started to resonate somewhat, but I didn't know where to go. I couldn't call my friends; I was too ashamed. I went to a local hotel and had the manager promise not to tell anyone I was there. On the third day, the phone rang and it was him. Apparently, not all of the hotel's employees got the message to keep my whereabouts a secret.

He said he was sorry and was full of fanciful promises. I didn't fully believe him, but I wanted things to work out. I forgot about me sitting sweaty palmed with a rifle ready to kill my mother's abuser. I went back to my apartment. The horrible memories during our relationship became too much, so I decided to move into another apartment. He continued to call and send flowers, but I would always refuse to meet with him.

In a weak moment, I agreed to meet him at a restaurant. While there, he went back and forth from arrogance to passiveness in an attempt to convince me that we needed to get back together. He was a master manipulator, and despite my distrust of him, I could feel myself being sucked in like quicksand. But as he walked me to my car, something inside of me screamed, "No, stop. I can't do this." That lesson from mother's situation during my childhood finally sunk in.

When we reached my car, I told him that I had a surprise for him.

"Really?" he asked.

I yelled, "It's over!" I emancipated myself.

My jubilee was short lived; as if possessed, he became quickly enraged. His voice got louder, his nose flared and his eyes widened. I'd seen this before. He was going to become violent.

I wasn't going to take it. Not again. Not ever again. It was time to flip the script. I opened the car door, got into the driver's seat, leaned over, and pulled out a gun. He took off running like his name was Seabiscuit. I followed him into the restaurant; the gun tucked neatly in my purse. He ran through the restaurant. My steps were sure and purposeful.

"She's got a gun!" he tried to tell people.

I shrugged off his charges, "What gun?"

He reached a pay phone located outside of the restrooms and picked up the receiver. Who was he going to call? Who can save you when the rapture is upon you?

I stepped patiently closer. Death was knocking on his door and today he was going to answer; he was without choice. He dropped the receiver and slowly started to step backwards toward the restroom. Surely, he didn't think a little thing like a restroom door was going to stop me. This was his road to perdition and I was the driver. Then, it clicked. "Am I really going to kill a man in a restaurant filled with witnesses while they are having lunch?" I thought, "Have I gone crazy?" I stopped.

I turned around walked out of the restaurant. If he was to go to hell, lucky for him, today wasn't his day. I got inside my car and sat still. It started with a snicker and then I had a good laugh. I couldn't believe what I had just done.

I called his mother. I told her that if her son ever came near me again, that she should have her black dress ready.

"Oh, baby," she moaned, "I thought you were going to marry him."

I laughed out loud. "I can't afford to marry him," I said. "I have one boy to raise to manhood. I am not raising two. You did a poor job with him. You can improve that by telling your son to stay away from me. It just may save his life. Good-bye."

I never heard from him or her again.

Logan's Lessons

If it looks like a duck and quacks like a duck ... you know the rest. Learn to harness and trust your own intuition. Bad relationships are mentally, physically and financially draining.

My advice is:

- Protect your financial and emotional wealth at all times!

- Keep in mind, if it's too costly to date them, you probably can't afford to marry them.

- It's better to be alone, than to be wishing you were alone.

- You can't see the picture when you are in the frame.

- Sometimes, we make money and relationship mistakes; learn, forgive yourself and move on!

CHAPTER 9

Sell The Vision

Trey and I outgrew the apartment. I needed a fresh start and he needed a place to run and play like other kids. I didn't need a financial expert to tell me that I was throwing money away by renting. I was paying $1,000 a month over two years which comes to $24,000 that I would never see again. It just didn't make sense to throw away that kind of money. John would not have been proud of me renting. It was time to buy a house.

With a keen awareness that no one was going to come rescue me, I resolved to do it myself. It was the start of my career in real estate. Like everything done without proper preparation, it started badly, but I muddled through. Even though I didn't have formal training, I knew my instincts would lead me in the right direction. Sometimes the best wisdom is learned in the streets.

I drove around in neighborhoods that felt comfortable, were close to downtown and had reputable schools. I saw what looked like a dollhouse and it caught my attention. It was located in a quaint tree lined neighborhood. It even had a peach tree in the backyard. I contacted the agent, made an offer and wrote a contract to buy. I didn't know what I was doing, and there was no one to advise me. I just trusted my instincts again.

Looking back, I was right on the house, wrong on the offer. There was a downturn in Houston's economy and houses were selling slowly. It was a buyer's market, and I was acting like it was a seller's market. Some houses in that neighborhood were on the market for over a year, which puts buyers in a better bargaining position. I offered the seller only 3 percent less than his asking price. He put many stipulations on the sale; he required that I close in 45 days and demanded proof that I could afford the house within 10 days. I jumped through every hoop he created for me.

I should have had him jumping through my hoops. I should have at least negotiated the price of the house at 20 percent less than his asking price. Secondly, I should have asked him to incur a portion of my closing costs.

For the second time, I found myself clueless at another real estate closing. We had the closing at a title company that was owned by one of my friends, I assumed she would educate me through the process. She didn't. She was focused on closing the transaction - not educating me about the intricacies of buying a home. Before closing on the house, I had tried to seek information elsewhere, but couldn't grasp the meaning of terms like prime rates, trusts, deeds, liens, and contingencies. I signed and initialed volumes of paperwork and was given the keys to my new home. We moved in immediately. In retrospect, I would have been better served had I used a realtor.

I had come full circle since John's death; Trey quickly adjusted to the new environment. He readily made friends, loved his school and enjoyed playing in the open spaces of the backyard. I loved the neighborhood conveniences. We lived in a great neighborhood. To my surprise and good fortune, within six months the real estate market began to turn upward and the value of our home increased. Despite my ignorance in the actual purchase of the house, my natural instincts for spotting a good real estate deal was confirmed.

Now, I was the owner of two houses. The first was purchased by John before our wedding, and it was converted into rental property in Chicago and, of course, my Houston home. The money from the rental property came in handy when it was time to pay my mortgage on my new home and other living expenses. This is considered passive income – money I didn't have to work for. Still, there was nothing passive about trying to maintain a house in Chicago. The winters there are hard on houses.

I increasingly had to take on the role John had once filled – that of landlord. When the house needed painting, mortar work, plumbing or electrical repairs, it fell on me to find the right contractors to fix the problems. I had a lot of homework to do to keep from being taken to the cleaners. As the mysteries surrounding home ownership cleared up, I began to fully appreciate the tax advantages my accountant spoke of.

Owning property is a tremendous responsibility. I could no longer ignore the fact that investing in real estate was extremely profitable. I had a rental property with $40,000.00 of equity and my new home was rapidly increasing in value. I wanted to learn more, so I enrolled in a real estate class. I waded through the nuts and bolts and came to one conclusion: If you have the ability to buy and sell to your advantage, and can see value beyond what was right in front of you, you can make good money in real estate.

I decided to get more involved in the real estate game just to earn extra money. I established a relationship with a local realtor who dealt with investment properties. He knew that I was a small time player, but he always kept me in the loop. One day he called about a small foreclosure deal that he thought would allow me to get my feet wet. He kept reiterating, "Marilyn, this might be a really, really good deal for you, but I suggest you really keep an open mind."

I thought, here's a perfect opportunity for me – a foreclosed condominium with a great location and a low price. I was excited and couldn't wait to see the inside. I met the realtor at the property. As we approached the front door, I asked "What is that smell?"

With a coy expression on his face, he said, "What smell?"

As he opened the door, a horrid stench greeted us. "Who died here?" I asked again. He ignored my question, and continued to show me the condo. I was close to receiving my real estate license and I knew he was required by law to tell me if somebody had died in the house. Fine, I thought. He wanted to play that game with me. This smell is too awful to ignore. Either somebody died here or skunks were the previous owners.

I followed him into the kitchen. Not only were the cupboards bare, but everything else, too. All of the appliances had been stolen.

When I stepped on the carpet in the den, my feet disappeared. I knew top grade carpet from buying it with John a few years earlier and this was top grade. I determined that no children had resided here because their little fingerprints would have shown up somewhere, like Trey's did on the walls at our home.

As we headed into the bedroom, I did a mental checklist:

No appliances.

Stinky place.

Good carpet.

Stinky place.

Clean walls.

Stinky place.

Large bedroom.

And then I saw it. There was a chalk outline of a human body that could still be seen in the hallway in front of the bathroom, along with a few dried bloodstains. I took a moment to register the sight. I thought, "Thank God he died in the hallway."

If he had died in the middle of the living room floor, I would have had to replace the entire carpet; it would have been difficult to patch the area with the existing carpet. His dying in the hallway meant I only had to remove the soiled spot and replace it with tile flooring. Although the walls were in good shape, I would repaint the entire condo because the paint would erase the smell. Even though someone had died here, the deal was very much alive. I didn't question the details of the death. All I needed to know was the condo's sale price.

The realtor told me the bank wanted $17,000.00. It didn't take a Rhodes Scholar to figure out the property had probably been on the market for a long time. I'm certain many people were shown the condo and were immediately turned off by the smell and the bloodstains, but my instincts were screaming grab this property. There were other one-bedroom condos in the area selling for $55,000.00. I knew there was money to be made here.

"Tell the bank I will buy this condo for $9,000.00." I told the realtor. He told me there is no way the bank will take such a low offer. I said, "just submit it." Reluctantly, he presented my offer. To the realtor's surprise, the bank accepted it. The property was off their books and on my hands.

I wasted no time getting it ready for tenants. I had the condo repainted. I spent approximately $3,000.00 on new appliances. I visited model homes for decorating ideas and saw how easily they created the illusions with decorating. I concluded that what people really wanted was a look.

To give the condo a fresh look: I installed stylish wallpaper in key areas, decorated the bathroom with accessories, and hung inexpensive pictures on the wall to give it a vibrant look. It was beginning to look like a model condo.

Prospective renters quickly appeared at my open-house. I managed to rent the condo for $250.00 more than any other unit to a couple who already lived in the building, which I thought was odd. When I asked them why they would pay me more for the same amount of space, they responded, "your condo looks warm, inviting and new." I realized in everything you sell, you're selling image as much as the product. I created an increase in the value of the property by simply changing the image of the property. Sometimes you have to sell the look instead of looking for the sale.

I eventually became a licensed Realtor and began working for a real estate firm. One day on my way to lunch with a co-worker, I saw a "for sale" sign in front of a house. I called the phone number on the sign and was told that the house was selling for $39,000.00. My appetite quickly disappeared. I knew, once again, there was money be made here, because a friend had recently purchased a home in the area for $145,000.00. I asked my co-worker to take me back to the office so I could write a contract to buy the house.

"Marilyn," he said. "You haven't seen the inside."

My blink moment told me, I didn't need to. The fact that it was a brick home with central air selling for $39,000.00 was more than enough information for me.

"I wouldn't recommend you buying a home without seeing the interior" he said. So I took his advice and we investigated this bargain. The house was smelly and dirty. Most of the rooms were in disorder; the kitchen was the worst. But, I saw through the ugliness to a well built house that had four bedrooms, 2-1/2 baths, and hardwood floors. It was déjà vu.

We raced back to the office and wrote a contract for the full $39,000.00. The house was in foreclosure and the bank wanted cash. There was just one hitch, I didn't have $39,000.00 in cash available. I had to think quickly. I told the bank I wanted to close in 45 days, knowing that was as far back as I could set it for closing. I had to flip the house within 45 days or I would owe $39,000.00. I wrote the bank a $500.00 earnest money check. The next day, I got a call from another realtor who offered to buy the house from me for $40,000.00. I laughed at him. He also saw value in the property, but unfortunately for him, he wasn't first to market. In real estate timing is key. When you see a deal you have to move with a sense of urgency.

I knew the house was worth much more than $39,000.00 and I planned to do minimum repairs. Time was of the essence. I had to move this house quickly. I needed to find a buyer before I closed on the property. I needed to do a double close, which meant the property ownership would immediately transfer from the bank to me and then to the new buyer - a buyer I had yet to find.

I had additional money available to renovate the exterior of the house. I had to transform the house from an eyesore into a block contender. I knew I was taking a big financial risk. I had control of the property, but I didn't own the property outright.

People began to come by to view the house and they were excited about the outside. However, once they went inside and saw the condition, their interest vanished and they all came out with "frowny faces." I was desperate for a buyer. The deadline was quickly approaching, when an attorney expressed interest in buying the house. He loved the outside, of course, but had reservations about the interior. I asked him to close his eyes while I painted an image of what the house would look like in 30 days after we closed. I took him through a mental tour of each room describing exactly what they would look like after the renovations. When he opened his eyes, I could see the excitement on his face, as he went from room to room. Then I heard the words that I was so desperately waiting to hear, "I'll take it," he stated. We agreed on a price, and he was the owner of the property just days before the bank called my note due.

At one time in my life I didn't even know how a garage door opener worked, now I was renovating properties and flipping them for big profits. My profit of $37,000.00 had been hard earned, and after all the renovations were completed, my buyer was one happy customer. I was really proud of myself and I knew John would have been also.

Logan's Lessons

I believe every one should have some type of sales experience. A sales job develops focus, determination and courage. No matter what profession one is in, you are always selling yourself.

My advice is:

- You should work a sales job at least once in your lifetime. The sooner, the better.

- The real estate game is tough. Listen, read, and learn before you play.

- Never ever buy a house at the top of the market.

- Your household expense should be about 25% of your monthly income.

- Don't become house rich and cash poor! Live below your means.

CHAPTER 10

The Student Becomes
The Teacher

I recall that I was 22-years-old, the first time someone put a name to my ability to motivate people to buy what I was selling. John and I were helping a friend sell t-shirts at a concert on Chicago's waterfront pier. I sized up the competition and quickly noticed that the other vendors sat in their booths and waited for potential customers to come to them. That didn't appear to be a recipe for success. I thought it made more sense to stand in front of the table and interact with the potential customers.

Our friend was a photographer and had a novel concept of instantly putting a person's image on the front of a t-shirt. Positioning myself in front of our booth in the line of foot traffic, I stopped all who came our way. "Excuse me," I said, making sure they got a good view of the "product" I was wearing. "Your face would look fabulous on the front of a t-shirt." I knew that giving individual attention would increase sales.

People responded to my tactic. If you sound confident and friendly, most people will do whatever you ask, the secret is in making an instantaneous connection. Our friend told us that he made more money while we were at the booth than at any other time. Then he looked at me and said the words I would never forget. "Marilyn, you are really good in sales. You are a natural."

Years later, the man who introduced me to the real estate business would say something similar, but in a slightly different way. "Marilyn, I hate you," he said, looking at me from across a lunch table. The hurt and confusion that showed up on my face prompted him to quickly continue. "Oh, no, no, no. Don't get me wrong. Let me explain," he said. "No matter what you do in life, whatever you touch, always turns to gold. You always land on your feet whenever you do fall. Why is that?"

If you fall enough times, like I had in my life, you eventually figure out how to bounce back quickly and turn a negative into a positive. As illustrated before, when it came to real estate, I certainly had the gift to connect with people and I was successful in getting a lot of deals done. I was never afraid to try something different and new when it came to getting customers and making the sales. Whether selling a product or a service, I knew these skills were something I could bring to any job.

My sales skills would be tested when I decided to make a career change from being a realtor to a financial investment broker. My friend Sarah, who was a financial investment broker, informed me that a position was available in her company. Although I was reluctant at first, she assured me that I would be able to catch on quickly. Sarah introduced me to the world of stocks and bonds, and with her assistance and guidance, I passed my licensing exam on the first attempt and became a licensed securities broker.

Her firm hired me, and I stepped into the world of high finance. Sarah was right, I grasped the intricacies of the job quickly, and I was making good money. My clients consisted of chief financial officers of banks and mutual fund managers. Shorthly after my first year, I made a $40,000,000.00 bond trade, which at the time was the largest institutional trade in the history of the firm.

I could have chosen a lifelong career in the world of high finance, but the long distance traveling that this job required took time away from my duties to my son and I didn't like that. Money is money, but there are other priorities in life. I chose to make my time with Trey as my number one priority.

It had been years since I had entered the world of stocks through condoms, as you may recall, but that was on the consumer end. I found myself moving from one financial sector to another. The travel demands of my first job were too taxing, so I decided to become a day stock trader, which allowed me to work close to home. It was a job with great risk/reward potential. If you make the right forecast, you could be up quickly and have a great day. I mean, literally you could make hundreds of thousands of dollars in a matter of hours – the reward, but on the flip side you could lose just as much in the same period of time – the risk.

My instincts for finding winners was working out well, in the beginning. I was doing extremely well and enjoyed the time I was spending with Trey. Gradually, I felt myself slowly becoming consumed by the business. There wasn't a second of the day that I wasn't thinking about the stock market. My winning streaks turned to losing streaks; dealing with the large wins and losses was too taxing for me mentally and physically. There were weeks when I was losing up to $30,000.00 a day.

Then, I had what alcoholics call a moment of clarity. One evening I saw an interview with a man who was a day stock trader as well. He revealed how his job was affecting his personal life and chipping away at his family. He would attend his son's basketball game and see a company's advertisement and wonder where the company had closed that day in the stock market. When driving his children around and one of them would mention the latest cool shoes he would start to think of where that company's stock traded that day. I immediately recognized me in him, and knew I had a major problem. I understood what addicts felt like. I had become an addict - a stock trading addict. It was all I thought about, and it was consuming all my focus. After a year-and-a-half of trading, I stopped cold turkey.

I had money in reserve, several career options – real estate, securities, trading – but I was at a crossroad. I had to find what was really right for me. What good is it to make all the money in the world if you're not on the right path?

It was a little unsettling not knowing what my next steps were. I forced myself to sit down with pen and paper and think about the perfect job for me. It had to offer a decent base salary with commissions high enough to outperform my salary at least three-fold. I needed flexible hours, full autonomy and absolutely no working on the weekends. One friend looked at the list of criteria and laughed. "You described a business owner." She stated. Her words would eventually prove to be prophetic. I soon landed a position as a financial advisor. I had an assistant and was able to delegate responsibilities, which made my job easier. We both took pride in our progress. I flourished rapidly. I was falling in love with the company. I contemplated throwing away my résumé. This was the perfect job for me, and I thought I'd never use my résumé again.

I had the opportunity to interact with individuals of various levels of employment and income. I discovered the inability to manage money did not fit a particular profile. Just because someone was a lawyer or had a MBA didn't mean that their personal financial practices were any better than anyone else's.

The seminars I conducted had people of all different nationalities, races and ages, but the one common denominator was their inability to manage their money. Many of the people I met were drowning in debt and living beyond their means. Most were a few paychecks from bankruptcy. Often times I would have people approaching me after the seminars asking for additional financial guidance.

There was one woman in particular that I took a keen interest in. She came to the front of the room with watery eyes and blurted out "I really need your help." The desperation in her eyes was intense. I pulled her to the side and asked, "How can I help." She began telling me her story. She was 56 and married.

Her husband was the head of the house and made all of the financial decisions. She recounted to me that she was having trouble sleeping, and was suffering from headaches and a nervous stomach.

"Why?" I asked.

"Because I am afraid that we are not going to have enough money to live on when we retire," she replied. She went on to tell me that she and her husband had recently moved from a house they had lived in for more than 20 years. They only had four years left to make monthly mortgage payments of $510. They moved to a much larger house with a monthly mortgage payment of $2,600. When I asked her if their salaries had increased to accommodate the bigger mortgage, she told me no. She worked for an oil and gas company and he worked for an engineering firm. That gave me an idea of their combined income, which along with their new mortgage payment and ages put them in a precarious position. She had reached the same conclusion. The only one who wasn't on the same page was her husband. She said he would never meet with me, because he felt that he was financially educated. I challenged her to get him to my office and I would take it from there. With tears rolling down her face, she said she would try.

Days later, the woman phoned, excited that her husband had agreed to a meeting. We wagered a dollar that once he came to my office, he would listen to my suggestions. She said she knew her husband would be in opposition, but she took the bet anyway. The next day, they came into my office and he immediately sat down with crossed arms and legs. "Show me what you got" showed up clearly in his posture and on his face. She quietly took the chair beside him. I began gathering information about them. He responded politely to my questions concerning their past and present financial situation.

The couple had three sons; two had graduated from college, the other was still a college student. I knew the tuition at that particular university was extremely expensive. I asked the husband if his sons paid for their education. With his chest stuck out, he responded, "No, I paid their entire college tuition - myself."

"Where did the money come from, sir?" I asked him.

"Out of my 401K," he replied.

"You had to pay taxes on that, didn't you?" I asked. "Well, yeah," he responded.

"So for every dollar you took out, 35 cents went to the IRS and 65 cents went to the university," I stated. I didn't wait for a response.

"Your oldest son is 28?" I looked down so that he couldn't read my facial expression. "What did he major in?"

"Liberal arts."

I put my pencil down and repeated the words "liberal arts" twice. "So what is he doing now?"

"Well, he's looking for a job," the husband said.

"Oh, I'll bet he's looking for a job," I commented. "And what about your second son?" I quickly asked.

The husband shifted in his seat as he answered, "Well he graduated already."

"Yes, and what type of work is he doing?"

"He's working for a temp company; you know, odd assignments," he said, quietly.

"Sir, do you personally know the president of the university your sons attended? Has anyone there ever sent you a Christmas card or invited you to their home?" The husband knew these were not questions I expected answers to, so he kept silent.

"You just gave your money away to total strangers."

"Did you attend college?" I asked, already knowing that he had.

"Well, yeah, and I paid for it myself," he proudly stated.

"You paid for college yourself, but you raised children who couldn't figure out how to pay for college without your 401K being depleted?"

"Why did you buy the new house?" I asked, my tone not as careful as before.

"I needed it for my children," he answered, not so politely anymore.

"What children? Those aren't children," I declared, looking at my notes. "You have a 28-, 26-, and a 19-year-old. They're grown men, adults." I was hitting my stride now. "When did you get your first house?"

"At 24," he answered.

"How did you acquire it?" I asked.

"Well, I financed it," his loudest answer yet.

The climax to the conversation was nearing. I leaned forward and looked directly into his eyes. "I must applaud you on how you personally chose to finance your education and your home. However, you have obviously neglected to pass this financial knowledge on to your sons. You have failed to teach your sons to be the heads of their homes; you are teaching them to be financial failures."

The husband was clearly upset. The color in his face had deepened a dark red. I wasn't quite finished with him, yet. He told me earlier that he wasn't putting the maximum deduction allowed into his 401K because his company's stock was lousy. That meant the IRS was taking more than its share of his income.

"You sir, are having a financial affair with the IRS." I asked his wife, "How does it feel to know that your husband loves someone else more than you?" Everything about her said fear. It was clear that she had never heard anyone talk to her husband like this, and she wasn't sure what he would do. Her lips stayed sealed as she sat in her chair quietly.

He was restless. His legs crossed and uncrossed. His body jerked backwards and forwards. His mouth opened and closed with loud attempts to explain. Finally, he had enough and told his wife they were leaving.

"Sir," I countered. "You are financially ill, and you don't want to hear it nor are you interested in any financial medication." He went for the door, but I got there first. I leaned against it and asked him if he was going to push me away from my own office door. His look told me he would rather strangle me.

I looked at him with all the sincerity I could muster from my soul. "Please stop this behavior, sir, you are ruining your family. You are financially killing yourself and your wife. You are the financial leader of the household. Would you please sit down and allow me to equip you with a financial plan to assist you out of this horrible mess?" I could see the fear in his eyes, I could feel his thoughts rambling.

He walked to the chair, flopped down, and with reluctance snarled, "So what's your advice?"

"First of all," I said, settling into my chair as his wife slid into hers, "you must get rid of that attitude. I am not the enemy. Second, I want you to go to the mall, buy a t-shirt and have 'I'm financially out of shape' printed on the front. When you leave my office today, don't go back to work. I want you to fully digest what I am telling you. The process is not going to be easy. For the next couple of months your pride and ego will have to be set aside. You will have to work counter to what your mind and heart will initially tell you. To become financially fit, you will have to shed the 'bad decision weight' you have put on over the years. Do as I recommend – and trust me, I promise, you both will be sleeping a lot better. You will experience financial peace. Now, get in your car and drive straight home and put up a 'for sale' sign in front of your home."

He tried to object, wanting to know if he could keep the house until the summer was over. I replied, "Absolutely not. You must sell that house with a sense of urgency and purchase a smaller home with a lower mortgage payment. Your two oldest sons need to either move out or contribute monthly to your household expenses. Start contributing the maximum amount to your 401K plan, and never again borrow against your retirement account." The wife called me the next day and thanked me profusely. Six months later, I received an envelope from her with a dollar bill enclosed with a note which read: "Glad I lost the bet; all your recommendations have been put into action. You gave us our life back. Thanks. I now have dreams instead of nightmares when I sleep." Somehow – by trial, error, necessity, gumption and common sense, I'd gone from being a woman, helpless and alone in the world, to one who could help people master their finances. I'd gone from passive to aggressive, and from timid to terrifyingly right. I was helping people in the way I once needed it – not by doing for them, but by teaching them to do for themselves.

There were thousands of couples and individuals who benefited from my unique style of no-nonsense financial advice. Most times, I felt like I was acting more in the role of a coach, trainer, and therapist rather than a financial advisor. I was helping them tackle their financial demons, making them face the myths, and breaking their bad habits about money. I was literally whipping people into financial shape and removing the financial friction from their relationship. It was the best feeling I had since before John left my life. I felt like I was passing on the gift John had given to me - financial freedom.

Logan's Lessons

Enrich your life by sharing what you have learned with others. Every new day can allow you to have a new experience. Be as eager about accepting information as you are about giving it. You don't have to be great to get started, but you have to get started to be great.

My advice is:

- Money conversations can be uncomfortable - get over it!

- It's never to late to learn a new profession.

- Don't allow someone to marry your debt.

- Hire a financial coach - to help you win the money management game.

- Learn it. Do it. Teach it.

CHAPTER 11

Fired Into Ownership

In corporate America, sometimes the light is shining bright on you and suddenly darkness appears. Even though I was one of the top producers in the company, when jealousy arises, you can become a target. The relationship with my manager was abruptly deteriorating. When I was dependent on him for guidance and information, things were fine. However, when I began to stand on my own two feet and move away from his influence, he became jealous, which was one of the contributing factors that lead to me being fired.

The firing literally turned my world upside down. I was more insulted than hurt and I needed time to heal my wounds. After a two-year hiatus from corporate America, I decided to return to the rat race. I dusted off my old contact information binder, put out a few feelers, sent out some résumés and set-up lunch meetings with executive friends. I went on some interviews, received a couple of offers, but nothing really grabbed me. I decided to meet one of my trusted friends to discuss my options. There are people in your life, at times, who see more potential in you than you see in yourself; he was one of those people. As we discussed my options, he quickly noticed my reluctant demeanor which signified my lack of interest in any of my job offers. He grabbed my hand firmly and looked directly in my eyes and said, "Marilyn, you have a natural talent for seeing value in real estate and you are an outstanding salesperson. You have used those talents to make a lot of money for others. It's time to pay the piper. Marilyn do you know who the piper is? The piper is you. It's time for you to be your own boss."

I leaned back into my chair and thought for a moment. He was right. I left that lunch meeting with a sense of calmness and clarity of direction. I had some experience in real estate, but I needed to increase my real estate knowledge if I was going to build a successful business.

I joined a real estate investment group which taught me more about single family and multi-family properties. I learned that there were many options available in the single family market from leasing, renovations, new construction to foreclosures. Each had their own complexities, but I was drawn to the foreclosure market. I discovered that the foreclosure market was tied to a person's lack of financial responsibility.

I had seen many situations, as a financial advisor, where people had purchased more house than they could afford. I was beginning to recognize the connection that my past had with my future. After gathering more information and data on the foreclosure market, I formed a foreclosure business which focused on people losing their homes due to illness, death, loss of job and/or marital problems.

My first successful foreclosure was a couple going through a divorce. They were so angry with each other that no one was paying the mortgage because they probably didn't want the other to get the house in the divorce. It's amazing what divorcing couples will do when they are angry at each other. This couple would rather let their home go to auction and ruin each other's credit than to find an amicable compromise. I was there to find a win-win situation for all of us. I went in and met the couple along with their three children. After taking a tour of the house, we sat on the living room sofa, he on one side, she on the other and me in the middle like a referee in a boxing match.

It was as if that signaled the start of round one. They didn't want to talk about their house going to foreclosure, which was the only reason I was there. Instead, they wanted to talk about their failed relationship and the irresponsible spending habits of each other. This family was obviously suffering from a lack of financial harmony.

My patience was running thin. It was 7:00 p.m. and I still had another appointment before my day ended. I tossed their file to the side. Silence abruptly took over the room. "Wait a minute, guys," I said, holding my hand up like a traffic cop. "I'm here to discuss the house going to foreclosure, and nothing more. I am not interested in knowing how you got to this point." However, deep down I knew I had to afford them my financial wisdom. Here was an opportunity for me to help them through a tough situation and potentially alter the direction of their family. They couldn't save their home from foreclosure, but I knew I could possibly help them save their marriage. It was clear that underneath the sea of frustration and anger, a foundation of love still existed. Their real enemy was the lack of financial direction.

I asked them a few questions to quickly assess their spending habits and income. They were not surprised to find out there was more money going out than was coming in. I told them in a matter-of-fact tone, "You can't financially afford to get a divorce." I recommended that they allow me to revamp their spending and made some huge suggestions that I knew would be uncomfortable, but necessary. I encouraged them to try my suggestions for six months and I would guarantee that their financial stability and marital bond would be recaptured. I took over their home and set them on a financial path with a clear sense of direction that would greatly benefit their entire family.

I have been a successful business owner for five years now. Being your own boss really does have its privileges and responsibilities. It has given me the financial freedom to enjoy the things I really love to do – skiing, golfing, traveling, and lecturing. Some people say money isn't all that important, but I believe it is. Don't make the mistake of underestimating its value. Simply put, money offers you options in life.

Logan's Lessons

Never, ever underestimate the financial components of the relationship.

My advice is:

- It's never too late to scale down and start over.

- Exhaust all avenues before calling it quits.

- The best time to look for a job is when you have a job.

- Always develop and keep a "side hustle." You never know when it will become your main source of income.

- Never, ever stop learning about money!

- **NOW, GET YOUR MONEY RIGHT!**

CHAPTER 12

Marilyn's Money Musts!

Just like losing weight, any goal begins with a purpose and setting a strategy of achieving a desired outcome. Those who become successful at it, do it through discipline, proper nourishment, and consistent exercise. There really is no secret formula to losing weight; consistently expend more calories than you bring into your body and you will lose weight—it really is that simple. However, in managing our money for the lifestyle we desire, the opposite is true; understanding the power of credit and consistently saving or bringing home more money than you spend, helps one build a nest-egg! Unfortunately, we sometimes get wayward and let the temptations—junk food in losing weight/ junk purchases in losing savings—distract us from our plan of success.

Change is never easy, but in order for one to get started on a new path of financial fitness, one must understand the **who, what, when, where, why** and **how** of money management. And for those who "have it under control," remaining vigilant about maintaining your financial fitness is paramount. Now that your "financial palates" are wet after getting the main course of *I Can't Afford To Marry You* and *Logan's Lessons*, here are some of my **<u>Must</u>** have money tips and "exercises" needed for changing your financial diets and whipping yourselves—couples and individuals—into financial shape!

Must know **who** is looking at your credit score!

- Lenders use it to determine if you are good at making payments on time. *Bad credit history = Bad interest rate = loss of Good earned money*!

- Insurance, utility, telephone, mortgage companies and banks use credit scores to see how responsible you are with your money; lower score equals irresponsibility in their eyes and thusly higher rates or disqualifications for loans. This results in increased cost to you on phone service, credit cards and insurances (car, house, renters).

- Companies, governmental and healthcare agencies use it to determine if they want to hire you! *Same qualifications, but your score is 500 and the other candidate's score is 750. Who would you hire if you were in charge? I thought so...*

- Landlords use it to check your rental payment history. They can charge more up-front money in securing your apartment or not offer housing at all. This may limit your options on where you want to live.

<u>*Must*</u> know **what** makes up your credit score! Your credit score is a measure of "credit risk" and is not based on income. A credit report is divided into four parts; identifying information, credit history, public records, and inquiries. FICO scoring is used to calculate your credit score and is determined by:

- <u>Payment history</u> – 35%:

  > Pay your bills on time; 30 day past due and "charge-offs" can really hurt. *OUCH!* – *Look at automatic bill pay as an option.*

- <u>Amount of debt owed</u> – 30%:

  > Don't max out your credit cards, big balances can hurt your score. - *Pay down cards that are closest to their limits! Keep your credit balances at about 30% of the limit. Example, limit is $1000 try to keep balance no more than $300!*

- <u>Length of credit history</u> –15%

  > Think twice before closing accounts! That credit account you have had for 15 years in good standing, <u>do not</u> close! - *If an old card has not been used for a while, make a small purchase on it every few months and pay in full. This can help your score!*

- <u>New Credit</u> – 10%

    It may be "cool" to flex that you have 15 cards ranging from Gap to Saks, but every time you get a new card you get a new "inquiry" on your report and these can ding points on your credit score. - *Don't apply for unnecessary credit! Avoid frivolous credit applications for about two years if you are looking to buy a big ticket item (house or car). Every point counts in get - ting that lower interest rate!*

- <u>Types of Credit used</u> – 10%

    This is comprised of the number and types of credit lines you have (car loans, mortgages, finance accounts). *Many couples want to buy investment properties; be wise in spreading your credit between the two of you. No need to tie up both credit profiles with one house!*

Must know **why** it is important to keep the best credit score! The FICO credit scale ranges from 300 to 850. A score above 700 gets the best interest rates and scores below 600 are considered high risk. Bottom line, your credit score is your "adult" report card and is a predictor of financial success.

- Thousands of dollars are gained or lost based on your credit score. Remember, the lower the score, the higher the interest rate which means the cost of the same big ticket item bought by one person may differ drastically for another as outlined below.

- Person A and B each buy a $100,000 house. Person A has a credit score of 720 and person B, a credit score of 580. Person A will have an interest rate three percentage points less than person B and will save about $75,000 over the life of a 30-year, fixed-mortgage. No one wants to throw away 75 cents let alone $75,000 dollars. - _It is okay for a quarterback to throw a football away, but it is never okay for anyone to throw MONEY away_!

- Car purchase $30,000
(48 month note)

Credit score of 580	Credit score of 720
Interest Rate –12.0%	Interest Rate – 6.25%
Payment – $790.00 (mth)	Payment – $708.00 (mth)

Interest payment over the life of the loan

$7,921.00	$3984.00
LOST: $3937.00	SAVED: $3937.00

A home and a car are two of the biggest purchases of your life, and one can clearly see that someone will save about $80,000 and someone will lose that amount in this example. *Which side do you want to be on? Give yourself a raise by getting your credit score right. This is money you could be putting away in your retirement account, children's education fund or seed money for starting your own business!*

Must know *how* to increase your credit score! Here is one tip you need to do ASAP!

- Open 3 separate credit accounts at your local credit union - credit unions are now open to everyone! Each account should be in the amount of $150.00.

> Step #1: $150.00 deposited in credit account.

> Step #2: Get a loan for $125.00 for six-month term.

> Step #3: Deposit loan amount in credit account and allow payments to be automatically taken out to pay the loan.

> Step #4: Repeat on Account #2 and #3 on same day.

- RESULT: You will have three loans paid-in-full and on time reported to each credit bureau on the 7th month and your score will increase. This assumes you are current on all other credit liabilities. Repeat the process as many times as you would like. It takes about 1 hour to set up at your local credit union. *Do this now!*

- Check credit report twice per year and dispute information that is not yours. Credit bureaus make mistakes and sometimes information from someone with a similar last name and/or social security number gets reported incorrectly on your report. Removing a "30 day-late" or "charge-off" that is not yours can add critical points to your credit score. *Be vigilant because identity theft is also rampant!*

- Keep your charges on credit cards under 30% of the limit. For instance, if you have a $5,000 limit on a credit card and want to make a large purchase of $3,000, divide the purchase between two cards. This will keep your balance below the 30% mark. *Creditors don't like to see a card almost maxed out!*

- Do not close old paid off accounts. *Remember, payment history and length of credit history equals 50% of your credit scoring!*

<u>Must</u> know **where** to find information that can help you better understand the credit and money management process in order to keep you better informed; the better informed, the better manager of money you become for yourself and your family.

Web Sites:

- <u>myFICO.com</u>

  In depth information on credit scoring and financial educational resource

- <u>Annualcreditreport.com</u>

  Free annual credit report site

- <u>Bankrate.com</u>

  Up to date interest rate information for every State (car loans, mortgage rates, investments, college finance)

- <u>401k.com:</u>

  Site with information on retirement and investment education. *Remember save early and often and put in the maximum amount allowed!*

- <u>Jumpstart.org:</u>
  Educational resource on techniques in teaching children about money and increasing financial literacy

- <u>Frugalliving.com:</u>
  Site with information living a frugal lifestyle

- <u>Credit Bureau Departments</u>

  TransUnion
  Phone: 800-680-7289
  Fax: 714-447-6034
  P.O. Box 6790
  Fullerton, CA 92634-6790

  Equifax
  Phone: 800-525-6285 or: 404-885-8000
  Fax: 770-375-2821
  P.O. Box 740241
  Atlanta, GA 30374-0241

  Experian
  Experian's National Consumer Assistance
  Phone: 888-397-3742
  P.O. Box 2104
  Allen, TX 75013

- <u>www.MarilynLogan.com</u>

<u>*Must*</u> know **when** to teach your children about money. If you do not teach your children about money, the credit card companies, retailers and "the Joneses" will! Kids have no real sense of money because everything has become plastic. Adults have credit cards and children have gift cards. There is no longer a "money tree," it has been replaced by a "plastic tree"! Here is a non-burdensome tip on how to teach your children money management.

- If the child is 10, for instance, give the child $10 in what interval you choose – (weekly, bi-weekly, monthly). Get four jars and label them *spending, savings, investing* and *charity*. This exercise allows children to see the tangibility of money and gives them an active process in respecting its value. *In this process, you and your child will learn and become more financially literate*!

- The break down of the $10 dollars is as follows:

  $2 or 20% in the savings jar
  $2 or 20% in the investing jar
  $1 or 10% in the charity jar
  $5 or 50% in the spending jar

Saving   Investing   Charity   Spending

Marilyn's Must Mantra

- Must not be afraid of personal financial truth!

- Must exchange credit reports and HIV test results before marriage!

- Must check credit report twice a year!

- Must increase my credit IQ!

- Must be open and share financial information with spouse!

- Must know the rules of my credit card and check interest rates every pay period!

- Must pay bills on time!

- Must keep balance low on credit cards!

- Must keep no more than 2 credit cards!

- Must not charge more than 30% of credit card limit!

- Must not just make the minimal payments on accounts!

- Must teach my children about money management or the credit card companies, retailers and friends will.

- Must live below my means and pay myself first!

- Must save 15% of after tax income and put the maximum amount in my 401k, IRA or Roth IRA!

- Must never cash out of my 401k and never borrow from my 401k! NEVER!

- Must make my money work for me - 401k, business owner, stock market, and real estate!

- Must pool money together with spouse and review family/individual financial goals quarterly and have weekly money meetings with family. *To me, weekly family meetings at home are equivalent to weekly staff meetings at work – everyone needs to be on the same page!*

- **MUST GET MY MONEY RIGHT!!**

Epilogue

My journey from financial irresponsibility to financial wisdom began when I was 19-years-old. I did not know the true value of money and its major pitfalls of mismanagement until the man of my dreams came into my life. John was more than a husband to me. He was a lover, mentor, friend, leader, teacher and partner.

I don't know where John got his financial maturity from. Maybe it was because he was a straight A student in math during high school, or his engineering training from Purdue University. I will never know for certain, but I am glad that he shared his philosophy of removing financial disharmony from our relationship, which was critical to our success. His love was not only about hugs and kisses, but was also about setting forth a strategy of intimately tying financial success to marital bliss.

In our marriage, financial discord to a large degree was exterminated. Remember, financial pitfalls hide behind savvy credit card promotions and one's desire to want more than they can afford; which means, everyday is a struggle to abolish these financial demons in an effort to keep your marriage/relationship ventilated and open. Financial strife frustrates people, can distort their marital obligations, turn the face of the marriage inward and ultimately lead to divorce. There is not a day that goes by that I don't think about John. He would be proud of me going from that naïve 19-year-old to now running a successful business. I have learned that money can either allow you to do things or keep you from doing things. What is your money saying to you? I am forever grateful to John for uttering six words that changed my life and put me on a path to financial freedom: **"I CAN'T AFFORD TO MARRY YOU."**

About The Author

Marilyn Logan is a mom, entrepreneur, author and speaker. She is on a mission. Armed with an "open–mouth policy," a pull-no-punches style, and years of experience as a successful investment broker, financial planner and real estate investor. Marilyn aims to help people change their lives by changing their financial and relationship habits.

Add savvy, common sense and fearlessness to the mix and it is no wonder that Marilyn has left a trail of significant career accomplishments. She shoots straight from the hip with humor and candor. Marilyn leaves the audience with financial and relationship wisdom that will enhance their lives. She shares the benefits of her experience and wisdom to radio, television and seminar audiences across the country. For more information, about Marilyn, or for seminars and speaking engagements, please visit www.marilynlogan.com or call (713)748-0540.

Please forward your book comments and/ or money questions to:
marilyn@marilynlogan.com

Thank you!

I certainly hope you enjoyed reading "I Can't Afford to Marry You." I have received emails from thousands of people sharing their stories of how this book has enlightened them and their families forever. Now, it's your turn. Please take a few minutes to share your thoughts of how this book has changed your viewpoint about money. In addition, you can send any money questions you may have to me via marilyn@marilynlogan.com.

Again, thanks for sharing this journey with me.